The Wheat-Free Cook

WILLIAM MORROW

An Imprint of HarperCollins*Publishers*

The Wheat-Free Cook

gluten-free recipes for everyone

:: JACQUELINE MALLORCA

This book is written as a source of information about the effects of foods, vitamins, and dietary supplements on the body. It is based on the research and observations of the author. The information contained in this book should by no means be considered a substitute for the advice of the reader's personal physician or other medical professional, who should always be consulted before beginning any diet or other health program.

The information in this book has been carefully researched, and all efforts have been made to ensure accuracy as of the date published. Readers, particularly those with existing health problems and those who take prescription medications, are cautioned to consult with a health professional about specific recommendations for supplements and the appropriate dosages. The author and the publisher expressly disclaim responsibility for any adverse effects arising from the use or application of the information contained in this book.

THE WHEAT-FREE COOK. Copyright © 2007 by Jacqueline Mallorca. Illustrations copyright © 2007 by Jacqueline Mallorca. All rights reserved. Printed in the United States of America. No part of this book may be used or reproduced in any manner whatsoever without written permission except in the case of brief quotations embodied in critical articles and reviews. For information address HarperCollins Publishers, 10 East 53rd Street, New York, NY 10022.

HarperCollins books may be purchased for educational, business, or sales promotional use. For information please write: Special Markets Department, HarperCollins Publishers, 10 East 53rd Street, New York, NY 10022.

Designed by Nicola Ferguson

Library of Congress Cataloging-in-Publication Data has been applied for.

ISBN: 978-0-06-111988-0
ISBN-10: 0-06-111988-1

07 08 09 10 11 WBC/RRD 10 9 8 7 6 5 4

For Chuck Williams

contents ::

The Wheat-Free Cook

introduction ::

I'VE ALWAYS LOVED COOKING, and baking in particular, so when I was told that I could no longer eat wheat in any form, I was taken aback. And the diet sheet I was given seemed calculated to bring on severe depression. Torn between outrage and laughter, I decided that if life had handed me a lemon, I was going to fight back. I'd cook it.

As anyone who is new to cooking without wheat or gluten soon discovers, it was a bit like exploring a foreign cuisine and using unfamiliar ingredients. However, being a food writer, I'm used to developing recipes, so I did have an advantage right out of the starting gate. Flours made from brown rice, quinoa, teff, chestnuts, almonds, and flax began to fill my freezer. Cakes, cookies, and tarts were no problem at all, and in fact often surpassed the originals made with wheat flour. Gratifyingly, foodie friends and associates—knowledgeable cooks with critical palates—all chorused the same refrain: "Jackie, this is better than the real thing. And lighter. Can I have the recipe?"

Bread was another matter, at least in the early days. Gluten-free flours lack structure: they don't interact with leavening to create a light, airy loaf. The gluten-free bread you can buy is appalling, so I kept trying and finally hit upon the idea of returning to the small, round hearth breads of old. They have a crisp crust that contrasts with the soft interior, and being made with whole grains in true artisan style, they're healthful as well as delicious. They are also very quick to stir together.

Day-to-day cooking doesn't need all that much tweaking to make it gluten-free. After all, it's just as easy to thicken a comforting stew with rice flour or cornstarch as it is with all-purpose flour, and sautéed chicken breast tastes much better when coated with a mixture of ground hazelnuts and Parmesan than it ever did covered in stale boxed bread crumbs. I've included a cross-section of recipes for everyday cooking and weekend entertaining that everyone at the table can relish, whether they're gluten-sensitive or not.

Cooking necessarily involves buying ingredients, and gluten-sensitive shoppers do have to become hawk-eyed label checkers. Wheat can turn up in the most unexpected places, like soy sauce, so you'll find a buyer's guide on page 4. Be aware that "wheat free" doesn't necessarily mean gluten-free. Happily, new labeling laws now coming into effect are making gluten-free shopping easier every day, and some chains, like Whole Foods and Trader Joe's, offer pamphlets listing literally hundreds of gluten-free groceries, from corn spaghetti to Japanese tamari sauce.

There is a world beyond wheat, and a very rewarding one at that. I have thoroughly enjoyed creating these recipes, and I hope that you—and your family and friends—will enjoy them too.

wheat allergy versus celiac disease

A wheat allergy and celiac disease are not the same thing. When a person has a wheat allergy, his or her immune system has an abnormal reaction to the proteins in wheat. In extreme cases, this causes hives, difficulty in breathing, and a fast trip to the emergency room. Other major food allergens include eggs, corn, fish and shellfish, milk, peanuts, soy, and tree nuts, any of which can cause similar symptoms.

When someone with celiac disease eats food containing gluten, part of the protein found in wheat, barley, and rye, it triggers an immune-system attack on the lining of the small intestine. The resultant damage, which prevents the body from absorbing nutrients properly, can lead to diarrhea, fatigue, nausea and weight loss, and of course, malnutrition. Many health professionals believe that untreated celiac disease—which often has no symptoms—can lead to osteoporosis, anemia, infertility, and cancer. A related condition, dermatitis herpetiformis, causes a distinctive weepy, itchy rash that frequently appears on the hands, behind the knees, and inside the elbows. Unfortunately, a dermatologist will rarely suggest that it might be caused by something you ate.

Up until quite recently, it took an average of eleven years to get a correct diagnosis for celiac disease, partly because symptoms vary so much among individuals, and because it was thought to be a childhood ailment rarely seen in America. That point of view is changing. According to a 2004 report submitted by experts convened by the National Institutes of Health, it is now estimated that celiac disease affects 0.5 percent to 1 percent of the U.S. population, or between 1.5 million to 3 million Americans. (In Finland, it's 2 percent of the population; in Italy, 1.2 percent and in northern Ireland, .09 percent.) Diagnosis is often difficult, as the symptoms can mimic other conditions such as Crohn's disease, or be ascribed to irritable bowel syndrome. Blood tests can reveal celiac-related antibodies, but an intestinal biopsy is usually needed.

Celiac disease is hereditary, though not all children of a parent with the disease will test positive. As with a food allergy, there is no cure other than avoiding the offending substance, at least so far. Still, this beats taking drugs with unknown long-term side effects.

Although those of us with a wheat allergy or celiac disease must be vigilant about what we buy and eat, we don't have to forgo favorites like pasta, bread, and cake. We can still eat well and entertain family and friends at the table, perhaps even better and more healthfully than ever before.

Dining out also requires caution. Generous friends and relations who want to cook for you but are uncertain about the, um, gustatory limitations are no problem—just give them a copy of this book! Fast-food chains are generally off-limits, as the majority of their offerings involve wheat in one form or another. In any case, the food tends to arrive in those kitchens prepacked, and the staff has no idea what's actually in it. But here too, government regulations that demand full disclosure are starting to come into effect. All those people diagnosed with celiac disease, plus millions of others with various food allergies, do have a certain amount of clout.

As celiac disease becomes better known among the general public, even chains are starting to offer gluten-free specials. You'll find that the waiters in established restaurants are generally most helpful if you ask their advice about the menu, explaining with regret that you can't eat anything containing wheat flour in the sauce (or dusted on before browning), bread crumbs, croutons, or pasta. Chefs are nurturing people by nature, and will usually make a big effort to take care of you—and gain a happy repeat customer.

the gluten-free shopper ::

If you're new to dining well without wheat or gluten, keep the following "do's, don'ts, and maybes" in mind when grocery shopping. (For mail-order suppliers of gluten-free foods and mixes, and useful contact information for gluten intolerance support groups and other resources, see page 211.)

YES

All fresh meats, seafood, poultry, and eggs; fish canned in oil, brine, or water; cured or cooked meats like prosciutto and ham; many sausages (but always check the labels)

All plain fruits and vegetables (fresh, frozen, or canned); plain fruit juices; fresh and dried herbs; dried beans, peas, and lentils; olives

All plain dairy products, including milk, cream, and butter. Sour cream, cottage cheese, and yogurt are fine if they contain no suspect thickeners.

All types of cheese (except processed), such as Cheddar, Swiss, Parmesan, ricotta, goat's and sheep's milk cheeses

Olive oil, canola oil, and other pure vegetable oils; margarine

All vinegars (except malt vinegar)

Tamari sauce, if brewed solely from soybeans

Chicken, beef, and vegetable broths, if they contain no hydrolized wheat protein or other source of gluten

Jams and jellies, honey, sugar, molasses, maple syrup, corn syrup

Plain chocolate (dark, milk, and white) and chocolate chips; pure cocoa powder

Plain nuts and nut flours; peanut butter

Tea, coffee, and pure hot chocolate and cocoa

Plain ice creams, frozen yogurts (check the labels), sorbets

Rice (all types: white, brown, converted, jasmine, basmati, Arborio, etc.)

Corn (cornmeal, masa harina, grits, cornstarch, polenta, precooked polenta rolls, tortillas, etc.)

Other Grains, Seeds, Roots, and Flours

Amaranth, arrowroot, buckwheat (kasha), flax, millet, potato starch, potato flour, quinoa, sorghum, soy, tapioca (manioc), and teff

Pasta made from rice, corn, buckwheat, quinoa, or any other gluten-free grain; Asian rice flour and mung bean noodles

Miscellaneous Ingredients

Annatto; citric, malic, and lactic acids; glucose syrup; guar gum; lecithin; maltodextrin (a corn derivative, unrelated to barley malt); plain spices; sucrose, dextrose, and lactose; baking powder, baking soda, and cream of tartar; pure vanilla extract; active dry yeast; xanthan gum

Wines, red and white; fortified wines like sherry; all distilled alcoholic beverages such as brandy, rum, Scotch, tequila, and vodka

MAYBE

Modified food starch research suggests that most modified food starch used in the United States is cornstarch, but some may be modified wheat starch (contact the manufacturer if in doubt)

Oats (oats are technically gluten-free, but may be contaminated with other grains; see page 13)

Mustards, ketchups, salad dressings, and flavored yogurts (these products are usually gluten-free, but always read the labels)

Pharmaceuticals (pharmaceuticals are usually gluten-free, but check to make sure)

NO

Wheat, and anything with wheat in its name except buckwheat (a misnomer, it is gluten-free), and any form of wheat, such as bulgur, bread flour, cake flour, couscous, durum, einkorn, emmer, farina, farro, kamut, matzo, semolina, spelt, triticale, and wheat bran

Bread, pizza, hamburger buns, cookies, crackers, pretzels, and other bakery items made from wheat, barley, or rye flour

Breakfast cereals, except those marked gluten-free. (Even standard cornflakes contain malt flavoring, which is made from barley.)

Pasta made from wheat

Foods containing modified wheat starch, hydrolized wheat protein, malt (flavoring, syrup, or extract), and malt vinegar

Meat, poultry, seafood, or vegetables that have been breaded or floured, or are served with a sauce or gravy thickened with wheat flour or marinated in a mixture that contains soy sauce or teriyaki sauce. This includes most frozen meals, fast foods, snack foods, and deli take-out items.

Canned soups and chicken, beef, and vegetable broths containing flour or hydrolized wheat protein, barley, or pasta

Beer, as it is brewed from barley. However, gluten-free beers made in the United States, Canada, Britain, and Australia are now appearing on the market.

Happily, gluten-free shopping becomes easier all the time. The number of manufacturers making gluten-free foods is increasing rapidly, and new research often shifts foods from the "maybe" to the "yes" category. For well-researched, up-to-date information about what's in that used to be out, read the magazine *Gluten-Free Living*—see page 210 for details.

gluten-free grains, flours, and other ingredients ::

WHEN YOU LOOK BEYOND WHEAT, there's a whole cornucopia of gluten-free grains, seeds, and nuts out there that have been cultivated since the dawn of civilization. Rice sustains more than half of the world's population, and along with corn is the most obvious and useful alternative to wheat. In addition, there's South American amaranth and quinoa, East African teff, Asian millet (revered by the ancient Chinese as one of their Five Sacred Grains and the most widely used grain in India today), and northern European buckwheat, which isn't wheat at all but botanically related to rhubarb. Nuts such as walnuts, almonds, pecans, and chestnuts make wonderful flour, as do dried beans. Even cocoa can be utilized as a form of flour.

I can't claim that this is a comprehensive list, but it does include those ingredients most readily available in the United States. Some grains are best when used whole in pilafs, others shine when ground into flour and used for baking, and most are good both ways. Nearly all of them are utilized as whole-grain flours, with all their nutrients intact, and provide healthful complex carbohydrates and fiber as well as good flavors.

As a general rule, it's best to buy nuts and gluten-free flours in small quantities and store them in the freezer or refrigerator. Being completely natural, they contain no preservatives or other dubious additions. It's advisable to buy gluten-free flours that have been prepackaged in a dedicated facility. Open bins in natural foods stores can be cross-contaminated by other customers using a scoop from a neighboring bin containing, say, whole wheat flour.

In your own kitchen, keep any gluten-containing products strictly segregated, and don't share hard-to-clean items like a toaster, or let anyone put gluten-free bread or crackers on the same platter with those made from wheat. Even the tiny amount of gluten present in a few bread crumbs can cause trouble for celiacs.

You can grind your own flours from gluten-free whole grains, but it may be more trouble than it's worth. I have an electronic grain mill, which makes more noise than the Concorde taking off. It used to send my late-lamented cat flying from the kitchen with her fur standing on end. It does a good job, but wafts flour over every surface. An electric coffee mill reserved for grinding things other than coffee is useful for reducing small quantities of flaxeeds or nuts to flour. A food processor simply whirls the former about, and tends to make nut paste from the latter unless you add rice flour or sugar. I don't blend my own supposedly all-purpose flour mix, as most breads, cookies, tart shells, and cakes require different ratios of gluten-free flours to be at their best.

almond meal/flour

Ground from whole almonds with the bran intact, this mellow, off-white flour is invaluable for cakes and cookies. It is available ready ground, but unless you can find a source with a high turnover—to ensure freshness—and reasonable prices (Trader Joe's is a good source), it's best to grind your own. An electric coffee mill reserved for grinding items other than coffee works pretty well. If you use a food processor, combining whole almonds with a little rice flour or sugar, subtracted from the other ingredients listed in a recipe, helps to prevent turning the nuts into paste by mistake. Incidentally, 1 cup of whole almonds weighs 4 ounces. One cup of ready-ground almond meal weighs approximately 3 ounces.

amaranth

A tiny round grain known as the "mother grain" in the Inca empire, *Amaranthus caudatus* is not a true cereal, although it's used like one. High in protein, calcium, iron, and fiber, the whole grains cook in 15 minutes or less.

arrowroot starch

Derived from the rhizomes of various tropical plants and generally used in North America as a thickener, this cornstarch-like product gives a glossy finish to sauces. Be cautious about utilizing it in cookie doughs, as too much will turn the baked cookies into cement.

brown rice flour, white rice flour

The all-purpose workhorse of the gluten-free kitchen, flour milled from brown rice is mellow in flavor, nutritious, and generally invaluable. White rice flour (not to be confused with Asian rice flour, a silky powder) is milled from hulled rice. When used in baking, both brown rice flour and white rice flour are usually combined with cornstarch, potato starch, or tapioca starch to counteract their slightly coarse texture.

buckwheat, buckwheat flour

Not wheat at all but a relative of rhubarb (the name is derived from the Dutch *bockweit*, as these triangular seeds were thought to resemble beech nuts), buckwheat is a hardy plant that manages to flourish in poor soils and inhospitable climates. Famously used in Russian *blini* (pancakes) and Japanese soba noodles, buckwheat flour is excellent in rustic flatbreads. The whole grains or groats are made into kasha, a dish that corresponds to an Arabic pilaf or an Italian risotto.

chestnuts, chestnut flour

The European chestnut, *Castanea sativa*, contains more starch and far less oil than any other tree nut, and makes a sweet-tasting flour. Once used by poor peasants in rural Italy for making hearth breads and polenta, it's more of a luxury food today. Whole chestnuts can serve as a starchy vegetable or a stuffing ingredient, or be turned into delicious desserts. They are available fresh, canned, frozen, vacuum-packed, and candied. For more information on chestnuts, see page 102.

chickpeas, chickpea flour

Ground from dried chickpeas, or garbanzo beans as they are also known, chickpea flour has a distinctive but pleasant flavor, making it a good candidate for breads but not cakes. Universally popular Middle Eastern dishes like hummus and falafel are based on chickpeas, and the cuisine of India would be poorer without them. Garfava flour is a proprietary blend of garbanzo and fava bean flour.

chocolate

Chocolate is derived from the seeds of cacao trees cultivated mainly in Latin America, West Africa, Indonesia, Malaysia, and the Caribbean. Depending on where they're grown, cacao beans, like coffee beans, have distinct flavor characteristics: fruity, floral, and so on. After harvesting, the beans undergo fermentation, when they start to develop their unique flavors, and are then dried and graded. Chocolate manufacturers roast and hull the beans to free the meat, or nibs. These nibs are ground into chocolate liquor, a thick, nonalcoholic paste of cacao butter, a form of vegetable fat, and vegetable solids. Unsweetened chocolate is essentially solidified chocolate liquor with a high percentage of cacao butter. Bittersweet, semisweet, and milk chocolate contain increasing amounts of sugar, so the percentage of cacao butter decreases accordingly. White chocolate is cacao butter (often mixed with some other, cheaper fat) mixed with lots of sugar, milk solids, and vanilla, and tastes of dried milk powder. Dark chocolate and chocolate chips with at least 60 percent cacao butter are the best choice for baking—and eating—for their rich flavor and silky smoothness. Ghirardelli's 60 percent dark chocolate is an excellent buy, the thin bars are easy to chop and melt, and both the chocolate and Ghirardelli's 60 percent chocolate chips give first-rate results in baking.

cocoa powder

Cocoa powder is made when chocolate liquor is pressed to extract about three-quarters of its cacao butter. (The correct spelling got mangled years ago.) The remaining solids are made into unsweetened cocoa powder, either natural or Dutch-processed. Natural unsweetened cocoa powder gives a deep, intense chocolate flavor to baked goods, and is the form I prefer. Good brands include Hershey's, Ghirardelli, and Scharffen Berger. Dutch-processed unsweetened cocoa is treated with an alkali to neutralize its natural acidity, has a more delicate flavor, and dissolves easily in liquids. Valrhona and Droste are two excellent brands. Both natural and Dutch-processed cocoa make good gluten-free baking ingredients.

corn, cornmeal, cornstarch

Corn, more often known outside the United States as maize, is actually a kind of grass with huge seed heads, or cobs. Fresh sweet corn in season is a treat; popcorn is a perennial favorite as a snack; cornmeal remains an integral part of American cooking in the form of corn bread, grits, and tortillas; and Italian polenta has now become popular. Eating corn with beans creates a complementary mix of amino acids that raises the protein value. If possible, avoid labels that say "degerminated" when buying corn products; you want the whole grain. When used as a thickener for sauces, silky white cornstarch gives a glossy finish. Particularly useful in baking, it helps to smooth out the slightly coarse texture of many gluten-free flours, but like its fellow starches, has little or no nutritional value. Cornstarch is generally interchangeable with potato starch and Asian rice flour/sweet white rice flour in baking.

flaxseeds, flaxmeal

According to nutritionists, flaxseeds are one of most nutritious plant foods on the planet. They contain more heart-healthy omega-3 oil than fish and more fiber than oats, and supply protein and potentially useful phytoestrogens that may lower the risk of heart disease and cancer, and strengthen bones. Fortunately, they also have a pleasantly nutty, grassy flavor. You can grind your own using an electric coffee mill (a food processor just spins them around, as the outer coating is extremely hard), or buy preground flaxmeal and store it in the freezer. Flaxmeal lends suppleness as well as goodness to gluten-free breads, as it's high in flax oil.

garbanzo flour

See Chickpea Flour.

garfava flour

See Chickpea Flour.

lentils, lentil flour

One of the few dried pulses that don't have to be soaked before cooking, brown, green and black lentils cook in about 35 minutes and make a tasty side dish. The little red ones are best for soup, as they quickly disintegrate. Various kinds of lentil flour are much used in India for making poppadums, those crispy wafers that complement curries so well. (Imported poppadums are available, but read the label to make sure they are gluten-free.) Lentil flour is good in flatbreads, and lentil flour "riso" makes a welcome addition to hearty soups.

manioc flour

See Tapioca Starch.

millet, millet flour

One of the first grains to be cultivated by man, perhaps 12,000 years ago, nutritious millet contains almost 15 percent protein. The leading staple grain in India, it is also popular in China, South America, Russia, and the Himalayas. It has a mellow, nutty flavor and cooks in just 15 minutes, but few people in North America are familiar with it. Much too good to reserve for birdseed, millet makes an excellent pilaf or grain salad, especially when toasted before cooking to bring out its delicate flavor. It also makes a good hot breakfast cereal with raisins and honey. Use the flour mixed with other gluten-free flours in breads and muffins.

montina, montina flour

Developed in Montana from Indian lovegrass, a hardy native plant that thrives in poor soils, this high protein grain yields good flour for gluten-free baking.

nuts, nut flours

A storehouse of vitamins, minerals, and fiber as well as being good to eat at any time, almonds, hazelnuts, pecans, and walnuts make luxurious gluten-free flours. True, most nuts are also high in oil, but it's the heart-healthy, mono- or poly-unsaturated kind. When nuts are ground, the flavorful oil content can take the place of butter in baking; just as the starchy part stands in for flour. Nutrient-rich peanuts are not true nuts but legumes.

oats, oat flour, oatmeal

Oats do not contain gluten, despite long-standing claims to the contrary. Oats, however, are particularly subject to cross-contamination by other grains in the field, or during the milling and packing process in a plant that also handles other grains. In a recent newsletter published by the Celiac Disease Center at Columbia University, readers were advised that multiple studies in Europe and the United States show that the majority of people with celiac disease tolerate oats. Reliably gluten-free oats are available by mail order from the Gluten-Free Oats Company in Powell, Wyoming, and Cream Hill Estates in La Salle, Quebec (see pages 211–12). Aside from the fact that oatmeal tastes delicious, scientific studies have shown that oats contain a special form of fiber, beta-glucan, found to be effective in lowering LDL cholesterol.

potato flour

This is a heavy, strongly flavored flour sometimes added to bread in small amounts. Don't confuse it with potato starch, which is far more useful.

potato starch

A silky white starch with a texture like talcum powder that's useful as a thickener, potato starch is interchangeable with cornstarch and Asian rice flour/sweet white rice flour for smoothing out the slightly coarse texture of whole-grain brown rice flour.

quinoa, quinoa flakes, quinoa flour

Along with amaranth, high-protein quinoa helped to sustain the vast Inca empire before the arrival of the Spanish conquerors, who banned its cultivation for religious and political reasons. Botanically related to Swiss chard and beets, the whole grains make excellent pilafs and hearty salads; the flour—used in conjunction with other gluten-free flours—is good in breads. Quinoa flakes make a mellow, high-protein addition to homemade muesli, stuffings, and meat loaves, and can be cooked like oatmeal. Most quinoa must be rinsed before cooking to remove the residue of bitter saponins, the plant's defense against insects.

rice

Rice, *Oryza sativa*, sustains more than half of the world's population. There are hundreds of varieties, but all of them fall into two main camps: Indica rice, which is dry and separate, and Vaponica rice, which sticks together. The former is fluffier when cooked (think of pilaf); the latter contains more starch and is generally gummier and creamier (think of creamy risotto or rice pudding.) Whole, or brown, rice contains complex carbohydrates, thiamin, riboflavin, niacin, phosphorus, iron, potassium, and fiber. White rice is refined, with the germ and bran removed. In the United States, most refined white rice found on grocery shelves is enriched with at least some of the nutrients lost during processing, but not the fiber. Converted rice is parboiled before refining, a process that forces some of the B vitamins into the endosperm so they are not lost when the bran is polished off, but it's still not as healthful as brown rice. Some round-grain rice varieties, like Italian Arborio and Spanish Calasparra, are especially good for absorbing flavorful broths during cooking while simultaneously retaining their shape. All kinds of rice are gluten-free, from Uncle Ben's to the exotic ones like Bhutanese red rice and Japanese black rice. Glutinous rice, spelled with an "i," is another term for sticky rice. It does not contain gluten.

rice flour, asian

Not the same product as rice flour milled from brown or white rice, silky white rice starch is interchangeable with cornstarch as a thickener, and as a mixer in gluten-free baking.

sorghum/milo

A hardy, gluten-free mild-tasting grain believed to have originated in Africa, sorghum can be utilized like oatmeal, and is available as flour.

soy flour

Like most bean flours, yellow soy flour has a pronounced flavor. A cheap source of protein, it is used extensively in the food industry in everything from frozen desserts to meat loaf. A small amount can be used in gluten-free breads, but it makes them dense.

sweet rice flour/starch

Milled from glutinous or sticky white rice, this neutral-tasting (not sweet) starch has a slightly sticky quality that can be handy for baking when used in combination with other gluten-free flours, as it helps to retain moisture.

tapioca starch

A favorite for bread baking when combined with other gluten-free flours, tapioca starch lends a chewy, slightly elastic quality. Also known as cassava or manioc and derived from a root, the whole "pearls" and granulated tapioca can be made into a milk-based pudding.

teff flour

Tiny, highly nutritious teff, the staple grain of Ethiopia and Eritrea, is now cultivated successfully in the United States. Available as ivory or brownish flour at some natural foods stores and by mail order, teff flour has a sweet, molasseslike flavor and makes exceptional gluten-free brownies, cookies, and gingerbread. It can also be cooked like porridge for breakfast. A form of millet, it contains over twice the iron of other grains and twenty times the calcium: one cup of cooked teff contains more calcium (387 mg) than a cup of milk.

wild rice

This is not a true rice at all, but the long, dark brown, slightly smoky-flavored seed of an aquatic grass indigenous to the Great Lakes region. A luxury food that is usually blended with other types of rice because of its high price and assertive though delicious flavor, wild rice has twice the protein and fiber of brown rice, but not as much iron and calcium.

xanthan gum

Derived from corn sugar, this white powder looks a lot like baking powder and is used in similar amounts, so an admittedly rather costly 8-ounce bag goes a long way. Invaluable in gluten-free bread baking, it provides elasticity and helps to prevent dryness and crumbling. A very small quantity also benefits shortcrust pastry and some cakes and cookies, which can otherwise be too fragile. It can be found in natural foods stores, including Whole Foods, some supermarkets, and on the Web via sources such as the Gluten-Free Pantry, and it keeps at room temperature.

Breakfast

GIVEN THE PREVALENCE OF BOXED CEREALS, toast, bagels, and doughnuts on the average American morning menu, going wheat-free sounds difficult, if not impossible. In fact, breakfast bars and muffins made with alternative grains are delicious, not to mention good for you. Rice Flour English Muffins (page 135) freeze well and can be thawed and toasted whenever you please; toasty homemade muesli is another option. A weekend brunch, when there's time to linger, can include indulgences like pancakes, warm apple crumble, or an almond flour coffee cake like Grandma never made.

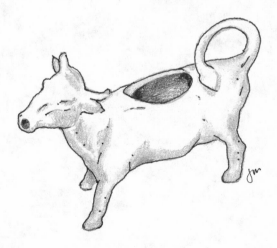

yogurt-rice flour pancakes

A GLUTEN-FREE BATTER makes exceptionally tender pancakes, and cooking them on an ungreased nonstick griddle ensures a fine surface texture. It also prevents the aroma of burned butter from permeating your kitchen. The recipe can be doubled easily.

Combine the rice flour, sugar, salt, and baking soda. In a separate bowl, mix the egg, canola oil, and yogurt. Add to the dry ingredients and stir until smooth. The batter will look thick and puffy. Heat a heavy nonstick skillet or griddle over medium-low heat, but do not grease it. Add the batter by the heaped tablespoonful, spacing the pancakes 1 inch apart and flattening the batter a little with the back of the spoon. Cook until golden on both sides, 2 minutes or less. Stack on heated plates or keep warm in a low oven.

½ cup brown rice flour
1 teaspoon sugar
Pinch of fine sea salt
½ teaspoon baking soda
1 large egg
1 tablespoon canola oil
½ cup plain whole milk
    yogurt

:: **Makes 16 three-inch pancakes**

rice flour crêpes

2 large eggs
Pinch of fine sea salt
Pinch of sugar
1 cup milk
1/3 cup white rice flour
1/3 cup cornstarch
2 tablespoons melted
    butter, plus extra for
    skillet

:: **Makes approximately 15**

UNLIKE A CRÊPE BATTER made with wheat flour, which has to stand for a while to let the gluten relax, this one can be used immediately. Quick to make and extremely versatile, crêpes can contain savory or sweet fillings, from Italian beef ragù (page 73) to applesauce. They can be made ahead and refrigerated or frozen.

1. In a blender or food processor, combine the eggs, salt, sugar, and milk. Process to blend. Add the rice flour and cornstarch, and process until smooth. Pour into a bowl and stir in the butter. The texture should be like thin cream. Stir occasionally while making the crêpes, adding a little water if the batter becomes too thick.

2. Heat an 8-inch nonstick skillet over medium heat, and grease lightly with butter. (No need to repeat this step.) Using a small measuring cup, ladle about 2 tablespoons of the batter into the pan, tilting the pan by the handle to cover the bottom. When lightly browned, about 1 minute, turn with a nylon spatula and cook for a further 30 seconds. Stack the crêpes on a plate with the well-browned side down.

3. To fill and roll, place about 1/3 cup of your chosen filling down the center of the paler side of each crêpe. Roll up like a cigar with the browned side out. Transfer to a plate or baking dish with the seam side down.

Brown Rice Flour ::

Flour milled from brown rice was once dismissed as being of interest only to health food fanatics, but its nutty flavor and healthful qualities now attract mainstream chefs. Unlike white rice, brown rice undergoes only minor milling. Just the outer husk is removed, leaving the healthful bran layer intact. Flour made from it has a nonintrusive, mellow flavor. When mixed with other gluten-free flours, it can make delicious breads with a crisp crust and a tender crumb. (But not always. Thus far, the leaden, presliced rice flour loaves available in natural foods stores could double as door stops.)

When it comes to making cakes and pastry, brown rice flour's lack of gluten becomes an advantage. While ideal for bread making, gluten can make other baked items tough, hence the use of low-gluten cake and pastry flours in upscale bakeries.

Don't confuse milled (ground) rice flour with Asian rice flour, a silky white powder much like cornstarch. The latter has its uses, but makes terrible bread on its own. On the other hand, for general baking, a small proportion of Asian rice flour/starch, cornstarch, or potato starch balances out the slightly coarse texture of brown rice flour very nicely. Tapioca starch serves the same purpose but adds a chewy element, so it's best used for breads.

Brown rice flour can be found in natural foods stores and some supermarkets, and by mail order (see page 211). White rice flour milled from polished white rice doesn't contain all the fiber and B-group vitamins, which are lost when the bran is rubbed off, but it's useful in certain baked goods and for dusting fish fillets or chicken before cooking as it gives crisper results than brown rice flour, which is softer due to the bran content.

Always store brown rice flour in the refrigerator or freezer. Being a healthful, preservative-free, whole grain flour, it can go rancid at room temperature.

rice bran and raisin muffins

1 cup rice bran

½ cup raisins

1¼ cups milk

4 tablespoons (½ stick) unsalted butter, softened

⅓ cup packed dark brown sugar

1 large egg

¼ cup honey

1 cup brown rice flour

½ cup cornstarch

1 tablespoon baking powder

½ teaspoon fine sea salt

½ cup sliced almonds, optional

Makes 14

TRUTH TO TELL, THERE'S not much difference between the average American muffin and a British cupcake. These muffins are of the more restrained plain variety, and are delicious with butter and marmalade. Like all muffins, they should be served warm. By the way, aluminum foil muffin cups will stand unaided on a baking sheet, and baked muffins don't stick to them.

1. Preheat the oven to 400°F. Grease muffin pans or line with cupcake papers. Alternatively, place 14 fluted aluminum foil muffin cups on a baking sheet,

2. Combine the rice bran, raisins, and milk in a large bowl, and let stand for 10 minutes.

3. Cream the butter and brown sugar together until fluffy, then beat in the egg and honey until smooth. Stir into the rice bran–milk mixture. Combine the rice flour, cornstarch, baking powder, and salt, and sift into the batter. Stir well to mix, and spoon into the muffin cups, filling them two-thirds full. Top with sliced almonds, if using. Bake until golden brown and risen, 25 minutes. Serve warm.

toasted quinoa muesli

MUESLI WAS ORIGINALLY CREATED in Switzerland about a century ago by Dr. Max Bircher-Benner, who served soaked raw oat flakes, nuts, and grated apple to patients at his natural health clinic in Zurich. A dear German friend, Inge Roberts, introduced me to her more luxurious version. She uses oats (see page 13 for more information on their gluten-free status); toasted quinoa flakes taste equally good. The recipe can be multiplied ad infinitum.

Combine the pecans, apple, and raisins in a food processor and pulse to make a chunky sauce. Add the quinoa flakes, and pulse briefly to mix. Divide between 2 bowls, and top with the sliced banana and yogurt. Drizzle with berry sauce or honey.

¼ cup chopped pecans or sliced, toasted almonds
1 apple, unpeeled, cored and chopped
2 tablespoons raisins
½ cup quinoa flakes, lightly toasted in a dry skillet
1 banana, sliced
1 cup plain whole milk yogurt
2 tablespoons berry sauce or honey

:: Serves 2

fig-quinoa breakfast bars

2 large eggs

⅓ cup canola oil

1 tablespoon dark molasses

2 tablespoons Seville orange marmalade or apricot jam

8 to 10 (4 ounces) soft dried Calimyrna or Black Mission figs, stems removed, finely chopped

¾ cup quinoa flakes

¾ cup brown rice flour

½ teaspoon xanthan gum

1 teaspoon baking powder

½ teaspoon fine sea salt

¼ cup sugar

½ cup (2 ounces) walnuts or pecans, chopped

∷ **Makes 12 bars**

KNOWN AS FIG ISAACS to my nearest and dearest, these nutritious bars are addictive. Like the Gingerbread-Flax Bars that follow, they freeze well and make excellent brown-bag fare.

1. Preheat the oven to 375°F. Grease the sides of an 8-inch square baking pan and line the base with parchment paper.

2. Beat the eggs with the canola oil, molasses, and marmalade until smooth. Stir in the figs.

3. Combine the quinoa flakes, rice flour, xanthan gum, baking powder, salt, sugar, and walnuts in a bowl. Add the fig mixture, and stir well to mix. The batter will be stiff. Transfer to the pan, smooth the top, and bake until light gold and slightly risen, 18 to 20 minutes. Leave in the pan for 5 minutes, loosen the sides with a knife, then turn out onto a wire rack. Peel off the paper, and let cool completely, right side up. Cut in half, then slice each half into 6 bars.

gingerbread-flax bars

ANOTHER HAPPY ALTERNATIVE TO commercially made breakfast bars, these bar cookies are reminiscent of French *pain d'épice*, or spice bread. Wrap them individually and freeze for breakfasts on the run.

1. Preheat the oven to 350°F. Grease two opposite sides of an 8-inch square baking pan and line the base and the other two sides with a sheet of parchment paper.

2. Combine the flaxmeal, rice flour, almond meal, tapioca flour, baking powder, baking soda, xanthan gum, cinnamon, allspice, ginger, and salt in a bowl. (If using whole almonds, combine in a food processor and process to a fine meal.)

3. Beat the canola oil, molasses, brown sugar, milk, and eggs together. Add to the flour mixture, and beat to combine well. Transfer the batter to the pan, and bake until the gingerbread is a shiny brown and starts to pull away from the sides, about 25 minutes. Leave in the pan for 5 minutes, then loosen the unlined sides of the gingerbread with a knife and turn out onto a wire rack. Peel off the paper, and let cool completely. Cut in half, then slice each half into 6 bars.

⅔ cup flaxmeal

½ cup brown rice flour

½ cup almond meal (or ⅓ cup whole almonds)

⅓ cup tapioca flour

1 teaspoon baking powder

1 teaspoon baking soda

1 teaspoon xanthan gum

½ teaspoon ground cinnamon

½ teaspoon ground allspice

1 teaspoon ground ginger

Pinch of fine sea salt

2 tablespoons canola oil

6 tablespoons dark molasses

2 tablespoons dark brown sugar

¾ cup milk

2 large eggs

Makes 12 bars

spiced apple crumble

3 or 4 (1¼ pounds)
Granny Smith or
pippin apples, peeled,
cored, halved, and
cut into ⅛-inch thick
slices

Grated zest of ½ small
orange

2 tablespoons fresh
orange juice

¼ cup sugar

2 tablespoons brown
rice flour

¼ teaspoon ground
cloves

:: Serves 6

THIS NOSTALGIC DESSERT MAKES a surprise—and always popular—appearance on a brunch table. Slicing the apples extra thin and tossing them in a little rice flour and sugar promotes an ideal texture. Start the crumble early: it has to cool down a bit before you serve it. Accompany with Honeyed Yogurt (page 29) or whipped cream.

1. Preheat the oven to 450°F. Butter an 8 × 10-inch ceramic baking dish.

2. Combine the apples with the orange zest, orange juice, sugar, rice flour, and cloves. Mix gently with your hands and transfer to the baking dish.

3. For the topping: Combine the rice flour, walnuts, sugar, nutmeg, and salt. Add the butter and mix with a pastry blender or your fingertips until the bits of butter are the size of small peas. Spread the mixture evenly on top of the apples.

4. Bake for 15 minutes, then reduce the heat to 350°F and bake for 30 minutes longer until the

topping is golden brown and the apples are tender. If it's not brown enough, slide the dish under a hot broiler for a minute or two. Let cool to lukewarm before serving.

honeyed yogurt

Whisk 3 to 4 tablespoons clear honey and ¼ teaspoon vanilla extract into 2 cups plain whole milk yogurt. (To make extra-thick Greek-style yogurt, see page 177.)

(To make extra-thick Greek-style yogurt, see page 177.)

TOPPING

½ cup brown rice flour

2 tablespoons chopped walnuts

¼ cup sugar

⅛ teaspoon nutmeg, preferably freshly grated, or ground cinnamon

Pinch of fine sea salt

8 tablespoons (1 stick) unsalted butter, cold, cut up

poppy seed and citrus loaf

8 tablespoons (1 stick)
  unsalted butter,
  softened
3/4 cup sugar
Zest of 1 small orange
1 tablespoon lemon
  juice
2 large eggs
2 to 3 tablespoons
  poppy seeds
3/4 cup white rice flour
1/2 cup cornstarch
Pinch of fine sea salt
2 teaspoons baking
  powder
Large pinch of nutmeg,
  preferably freshly
  grated
2 tablespoons milk

⁘ Serves 8 to 12

THIS RECIPE MAKES EITHER one loaf cake or a dozen tender muffins that can be frozen and reheated. It's best to buy poppy seeds in bulk at a natural foods store and keep them in the freezer, where they won't go stale or rancid. Buying them in little glass spice bottles is surprisingly expensive.

1. Preheat the oven to 350°F. Grease an 8 × 4-inch loaf pan and line the base with parchment paper. (Alternatively, grease a 12-cup muffin pan or arrange 12 fluted aluminum foil muffin cups on a baking sheet.)

2. In a large bowl, beat the butter and sugar until light and fluffy. Grate the zest off the orange right into the bowl, to catch the aromatic spray of orange oil. Add the lemon juice. Beat in the eggs one at a time, then add the poppy seeds.

3. Combine the rice flour, cornstarch, salt, baking powder, and nutmeg. Beat into the batter a little at a

time until smooth. Beat in the milk. Spoon into the loaf pan, smooth the top, and cut a trench down the center to minimize cracking. Bake until lightly browned and an inserted toothpick emerges clean, about 35 minutes. Leave in the pan for 10 minutes before unmolding, and let cool right side up on a wire rack. (If making muffins, bake until golden, about 22 minutes.)

almond-plum rice flour coffee cake

10 soft pitted prunes,
   cut in quarters
Zest of ½ lemon, cut in
   ½-inch wide strips
¾ cup sugar
4 large eggs
1 cup almond meal
   (or ⅔ cup whole
   almonds)
½ cup brown rice flour
½ teaspoon baking
   powder
Confectioners' sugar

:: **Serves 10**

PRUNES HAVE COME UP in the world. They are now referred to, by the Sunsweet growers in California at any rate, as dried plums. Whatever you choose to call them, prunes are generously endowed with fiber and potassium, and they make this rich-tasting but butterless cake moist and naturally sweet.

1. Heat the oven to 350°F. Butter the sides of a 9-inch round cake pan, and line the base with a circle of parchment paper.

2. Place the prunes, lemon zest, and 2 tablespoons of the sugar in a food processor. Process until evenly ground. Add 1 of the eggs and process to blend, scraping down the bowl as needed.

3. Mix the almond meal, rice flour, and baking powder together, and set aside. (If using whole almonds, combine in a food processor and process to a fine meal.)

4. Combine the remaining 3 eggs and sugar in a bowl. Beat at high speed to the thick ribbon stage, 7 minutes.

5. Using a rubber spatula, spoon half the prune mixture around the edge of the bowl and fold in, followed by half the flour mixture. Repeat with the remainder. (Just dumping it all on top would deflate the batter.) Transfer to the prepared pan, smooth the top, and bake until the cake is golden and shrinks away slightly from the edge of the pan and an inserted toothpick emerges clean, 30 minutes. Let cool in the pan for 5 minutes, then unmold and peel off the baking parchment. Let cool, right side up, on a wire rack. Dust with confectioners' sugar before serving.

Eggs and Cheese

FOR SATISFYING, OFF-THE-SHELF, GLUTEN-FREE MEALS, consider the egg. Perfectly packaged by Mother Nature, eggs will keep refrigerated for a month after the lay date, they're rich in protein and vitamins, and they team beautifully with cheese. All cheeses are gluten-free (except processed cheese, which can have all kinds of odd ingredients), with Parmigiano-Reggiano, cave-aged Swiss Gruyère, and sharp Cheddar topping my list of favorites for cooking.

creamy tomato and egg curry

THIS VEGETARIAN DISH HAS lots of flavor and is a great standby when there's no time for grocery shopping. Crispy imported Indian lentil flour poppadums make the perfect foil, and can be heated and puffed in a microwave oven. (They are traditionally gluten-free, but check the label.) Look for aromatic cardamom seeds in the spice department of a supermarket or natural foods store. They come encased in white or green pods.

1. Heat the canola oil in a skillet over medium heat until it shimmers. Add the onions and cook, stirring often, until translucent and starting to turn golden, 7 minutes. Stir in the garlic, curry powder, and cardamom seeds, and cook for 30 seconds until fragrant. Add the tomatoes, including the juice, the garbanzo beans, and ¾ cup water. Bring to a boil, reduce the heat to low, and simmer, uncovered, to form a thick sauce, 20 minutes. Add a little more water if the sauce appears to be drying out. Remove from the heat, taste, and add salt if needed. Stir in the yogurt.

2. Shell and halve the eggs, and gently stir into the sauce. Serve with rice, chutney, and poppadums, if using.

1 tablespoon canola oil
2 onions (about 6 ounces each), halved and thinly sliced
2 garlic cloves, thinly sliced
2 teaspoons curry powder or to taste
¼ teaspoon cardamom seeds
1 can (14½ ounces) diced tomatoes
1 cup cooked or canned garbanzo beans, rinsed and drained
Fine sea salt, optional
½ cup plain whole milk yogurt, at room temperature
8 large eggs, hard boiled
Cooked long-grain white rice
Mango or peach chutney
Warm poppadums, optional

Serves 4

Perfectly Cooked Hard-Boiled Eggs

Place the eggs in a saucepan, cover with cold water, and bring to a boil. Cover the pan, remove from the heat, and let stand for 12 minutes. The yolks as well as the whites will be firm all the way through, and just right.

goat cheese and potato open-faced omelet

YOU'LL NEED LEFTOVER BOILED potatoes for this creamy omelet, which can be tossed together in a few minutes. The skillet bread on page 143 and a green salad go well here.

1. Beat the eggs in a large bowl and set aside. Heat the olive oil in a 10-inch ovenproof skillet over medium heat, and fry the potatoes and onion until golden, 6 to 7 minutes. Add the garlic, and cook for 1 minute. Remove from the heat, stir in the bell peppers and parsley, and let cool for 5 minutes. Tip into the beaten eggs, stirring to separate the potato slices, and season with salt and pepper. Preheat the broiler.

2. Return the skillet to medium-low heat, add the butter, and heat until foaming. Pour in the egg mixture and cook undisturbed for 3 minutes. Top with the goat cheese, and slide under the broiler for 1 to 2 minutes, or until the eggs are just set on top.

Don't overcook or the cheese becomes tough. Garnish with basil, if using.

6 large eggs

1 tablespoon extra virgin olive oil

2 medium red or white potatoes, peeled, boiled, and sliced, cold

1 small onion, finely chopped

1 garlic clove, minced

3 tablespoons roasted, peeled, and chopped red bell peppers (from a jar is fine)

2 tablespoons chopped parsley

Fine sea salt and freshly ground black pepper

1 tablespoon unsalted butter

6 ounces soft white goat cheese, cut in chunks

Torn-up basil leaves, optional

:: **Serves 4**

parmesan puffs

½ cup brown rice flour
⅓ cup tapioca starch
½ teaspoon fine sea salt
1 cup milk
4 tablespoons unsalted
   butter, cut up
2 large eggs
½ cup grated
   Parmigiano-Reggiano

:: **Makes 20**

ALWAYS POPULAR WITH GUESTS, these savory puffs are crisp on the outside with a soft, almost hollow interior. Based on gougère, a traditional Burgundian snack, this gluten-free version makes an appetizing accompaniment to a glass of wine, and the puffs are delicious served in lieu of bread with a salad. It's easiest and quickest to form the puffs with a cone-shaped pastry bag, but you can also use two spoons.

1. Preheat the oven to 400°F. Line a large baking sheet with parchment paper. Have ready a decorating bag fitted with a ½-inch plain tip.

2. Combine the rice flour, tapioca starch, and salt, and set aside.

3. In a heavy saucepan, heat the milk and butter over medium heat just until boiling. Add the flour mixture all at once, and stir vigorously until the mixture clears the sides of the pan and forms a ball. Keep stirring for 1 minute, evaporating as much moisture as possible without scorching the paste. Remove from the heat. Add the eggs one at a time, beating hard after each addition until the mixture is smooth again. Beat in the Parmesan.

4. Transfer the mixture to the decorating bag and pipe 1¼-inch mounds on the baking sheet. Place in the oven and turn the heat down to 375°F. Bake until puffed and golden, about 25 minutes. Turn off the heat, and leave the puffs in the oven for another 5 to 10 minutes, with the door partially open. (Wedge with a wooden spoon handle if necessary.) Serve warm. Baked puffs may be frozen.

USING A PASTRY/DECORATING BAG

Fixtures in any professional kitchen for forming choux puffs, éclairs, and other small pastries, pastry bags can be found in any kitchenware shop, along with metal tips. To fill a pastry bag, insert the tip, then stand the bag in a tall jar. Fold back the top like a cuff, which you unfold when the bag is half full so you can twist the bag shut without the filling escaping from the wrong end. Chefs use the large, virtually indestructible canvas kind as opposed to the small, disposable variety. Choose a canvas bag, turn it inside out, and wash under warm running water as soon as possible after forming choux dough or it will be tiresome to clean.

onion-gruyère tart

8-inch Rice Flour Tart
Shell (page 169; made
without sugar), half-
baked
1 tablespoon unsalted
butter
2 onions (about 6
ounces each), halved
and thinly sliced
Pinch of nutmeg,
preferably freshly
grated
Fine sea salt and freshly
ground black pepper
2 large egg yolks
½ cup heavy cream
¾ cup (3 ounces) grated
Gruyère cheese
8 oil-cured black olives,
pitted and halved

:: **Serves 6 to 8**

BAKING THIS SAVORY TART on a pre-
heated baking sheet not only gets the pastry off to
a good start, but catches any errant spills. Serve
warm as a first course. Be patient when cooking
the onions: they have to simmer until they practi-
cally melt, but the wait is worth it.

1. While the half-baked tart shell cools, prepare the
filling.

2. Melt the butter in a heavy saucepan over medium-low
heat. Add the onions, cover, reduce the heat to low, and
cook, stirring occasionally, until pale gold and meltingly
tender, about 35 minutes. Season to taste with nutmeg,
salt, and pepper.

3. Preheat the oven to 350°F, and heat a baking sheet at the same time.

4. Whisk the egg yolks and cream together, and stir in the onions. Spread half the grated cheese over the pastry shell, spoon the onion mixture over it, and sprinkle with the remaining cheese. Arrange the olives at random on top. Place the tart pan on the hot baking sheet. Bake until dappled gold and the filling is just set, about 30 minutes. Let cool for 10 minutes before unmolding and slicing.

STORING FIRM CHEESES

Cheeses such as Cheddar, Gruyère, and Parmesan will keep better if wrapped in parchment paper, put in a plastic bag that's left slightly open, and refrigerated. This way, they get important air circulation, but not so much that they quickly dry out. When wrapped in plastic alone, cheese soon develops mold. A soft, fully ripened cheese, such as Brie or Camembert, won't keep no matter what you do to it, so buy only what you can use within a day or two.

spinach and zucchini frittata

2 tablespoons extra
  virgin olive oil
1/4 cup finely chopped
  onion
3 cups (8 ounces) loose-
  pack frozen spinach
4 large eggs
1 1/4 cups shredded
  Asiago, Pecorino,
  provolone, or Gruyère
  cheese, or a mixture
1/4 cup grated
  Parmigiano-Reggiano
1 cup thinly sliced
  zucchini
Fine sea salt and freshly
  ground black pepper
1 cup cooked, sliced, cold
  potatoes, peeled, or 1/4
  cup pecans, chopped

:: **Serves 6**

YOU CAN ENJOY THIS vegetarian frittata hot, warm, or cold for lunch or supper, or as an appetizer with a glass of wine. It's also perfect for a potluck party: it travels well. You'll need left-over potatoes to make this dish—boiled or baked work equally well—or you can stir in pecans for a crunchy contrast. Almost any cheese, including Cheddar or crumbled feta, works well.

1. Preheat the oven to 350°F. Grease an 8 × 10 × 2-inch baking dish with 2 teaspoons of the olive oil.

2. Heat the remaining olive oil in a skillet over medium heat, and add the onion. Cook until translucent, stirring, about 3 minutes. Add the spinach and cook, stirring often, until thawed, about 5 minutes. Set aside.

3. In a large bowl, beat the eggs lightly. Stir in the shredded cheese and all but 1 tablespoon of the Parmesan. Gently stir in the zucchini. Season with salt and pepper (remember, the cheeses contain salt). Spoon half the mixture into the baking dish, and top with the potato slices. Cover with the remaining spinach mixture, and smooth the top. Sprinkle with the remaining tablespoon of Parmesan. Bake until a dappled golden brown on top, 35 to 40 minutes. The texture will be firm rather than soufflélike. Let cool for at least 10 minutes before cutting and serving.

sun-dried tomato and parmesan soufflé

SOUFFLÉS PROBABLY EARNED THEIR reputation for being difficult to make before the days of electric mixers and ovens with thermostats. Actually they are very easy to produce; the only caveat is that diners must wait for the soufflé, not the other way round, as it does fall quickly. This version uses rice flour in the basic mixture.

1. Preheat the oven to 375°F. Grease a 1-quart soufflé dish with 1 tablespoon of the butter, and dust with 2 tablespoons of the Parmesan.

2. Melt the remaining 2 tablespoons butter in a heavy saucepan. Stir in the rice flour to make a smooth paste. Immediately add the hot milk and stir vigorously until the mixture boils. Reduce the heat to low and simmer, stirring constantly, until smooth and thick, about 3 minutes. Remove from the heat, and beat in the Gruyère and remaining 2 tablespoons Parmesan. Beat in the egg yolks, one at a time. Stir in the chopped sun-dried tomatoes. Season to taste with salt and pepper.

3. Beat the egg whites until stiff but not dry. Stir one large spoonful into the cheese mixture, to loosen it. Using a rubber spatula, fold in the remaining egg whites, using a cutting-down and scooping-up motion while rotating the bowl with your other hand. Transfer to the prepared

3 tablespoons unsalted butter, softened
4 tablespoons grated Parmigiano-Reggiano
2 tablespoons brown rice flour
1 cup whole milk, heated until tiny bubbles form around the edge of the pan
1 cup coarsely grated Gruyère
4 large eggs, separated
2 tablespoons drained and chopped sun-dried tomatoes in oil
Fine sea salt and freshly ground white pepper

:: Serves 4

soufflé dish. Using the spatula, cut a circular trench through the mixture about 2 inches from the sides of the dish, which helps the soufflé to rise evenly and form a "hat." Bake until puffed and golden brown, about 25 minutes. Serve immediately.

Vegetables and Grains

ALL VEGETABLES AND PULSES—from asparagus to zucchini—are gluten-free, but grains are another matter. For the gluten-sensitive, wheat, barley, and rye must be avoided like the Titanic with another chance. Still, other interesting choices vie for the cook's attention, and the wider the selection of vegetables and whole grains you use, the better for everybody's general health. Dried beans, lentils, corn, and rice are familiar staples, but quinoa and millet can make fans out of the most suspicious diner when offered as a pilaf or grain salad.

corn fritters

USE FRESH OR FROZEN corn kernels for these crispy, Asian-style fritters, which make a savory appetizer or a light lunch with salad greens. Some brands of tamari sauce are wheat-free, as is Thai fish sauce, but check the labels to make sure.

1. Break the eggs into a bowl, and beat lightly. Add the green onions, bell peppers, pepper flakes, tamari sauce, fish sauce, salt, pepper, and corn. Stir in the rice flour.

2. Heat the corn oil in a large nonstick skillet over medium heat until it shimmers. Drop in heaped tablespoons of the batter, and fry until golden brown on both sides, about 3 minutes. Put on paper towels to drain, and keep warm while cooking the remaining batter. Sprinkle with sesame oil and garnish with cilantro.

2 large eggs

4 green onions, white and pale green part only, thinly sliced

2 tablespoons roasted, peeled, and chopped red bell peppers (from a jar is fine)

¼ to ½ teaspoon dried red pepper flakes

1 tablespoon wheat-free tamari sauce, such as Organic San-J Tamari

2 teaspoons Thai fish sauce

Fine sea salt and freshly ground black pepper

2 cups corn kernels, thawed if frozen

½ cup brown rice flour

2 tablespoons corn oil

Toasted sesame oil

Cilantro sprigs

∷ **Makes 16**

zucchini fritters

½ cup grated Asiago or
  Parmigiano-Reggiano
¼ cup brown rice flour
1 large egg
½ teaspoon chopped
  fresh oregano or
  thyme, or ¼ teaspoon
  dried, optional
2 to 3 medium zucchini,
  sliced ¼ inch thick
2 tablespoons extra
  virgin olive oil
Fine sea salt and freshly
  ground black pepper

:: Serves 4

THIS IS A TASTY appetizer or side dish that cooks in 5 minutes. Long, slender purple or lavender Japanese eggplants can be substituted; like zucchini, their skins are so tender that they don't need peeling. Either one makes first-rate finger food with a glass of wine.

1. Combine the cheese and rice flour. Break the egg into a wide, shallow dish and beat lightly. Add the oregano, if using. Add the zucchini slices to the beaten egg, turning to coat well.

2. Heat the olive oil in a large nonstick skillet over medium heat until it shimmers. Meanwhile, place the zucchini slices on the cheese-flour mixture, then turn to coat the second side. Fry until tender and golden brown on both sides, about 4 minutes. (If cooking in batches, place on a plate lined with paper towels and keep warm in a low oven.) Season to taste with salt and pepper, and serve warm.

lentils with chickpeas

UNLIKE DRIED BEANS, LENTILS don't need soaking before you cook them. For my money, green lentils have by far the best texture; brown ones can be floury when cooked, and tiny red lentils turn to mush the moment your back is turned (they're good in soup, though). As with cooked quinoa, any leftovers can be turned into an excellent grain salad by adding a splash of wine vinegar and more olive oil.

1. In a large saucepan, combine the lentils, onion, garlic, parsley, salt, and 4 cups water. Bring to a boil, reduce the heat, and simmer until tender, about 30 minutes.

2. Drain, reserving the liquid. Return the lentils to the saucepan with ½ cup of the cooking liquid. Add the chickpeas, olive oil, cumin, and black pepper to taste. Heat gently, and taste for seasoning. Serve hot, drizzled with additional olive oil.

¾ cup green lentils, picked over and rinsed

1 medium onion, chopped

1 garlic clove, minced

¼ cup chopped parsley

¾ teaspoon fine sea salt

1 cup cooked or canned chickpeas, rinsed and drained

¼ cup extra virgin olive oil, plus additional for drizzling

¼ teaspoon ground cumin

Freshly ground black pepper

:: Serves 4

quinoa pilaf with red peppers

2 cups gluten-free
    vegetable broth or
    chicken broth
1 cup yellow quinoa,
    rinsed and drained
2 tablespoons extra
    virgin olive oil
½ cup chopped onion
½ cup destringed and
    chopped celery
1 garlic clove, minced
1 large red bell pepper,
    broiled and peeled
    (see page 53),
    chopped
2 tablespoons chopped
    parsley
Fine sea salt and freshly
    ground black pepper

:: Serves 4

AS VERSATILE AS WHITE rice but much higher in nutrients, quinoa cooks in just 15 minutes. It has a mellow flavor and a texture somewhat like caviar: there's a pleasant little pop to it between your teeth. The seeds grow in a multitude of colors, including white, yellow, pink, red, black, and orange, but the two you're most likely to find in the United States are light yellow and red.

1. Bring the broth to a boil over high heat. Add the quinoa, reduce the heat to low, cover, and simmer until the grains are tender and the liquid is absorbed, about 15 minutes. The grains will turn transparent, and the white germ ring will show.

2. Meanwhile, heat the olive oil in a large skillet over medium heat until it shimmers. Add the onion and celery, and sauté until softened, about 5 minutes. Add the garlic and bell pepper, and cook for 2 minutes more. Stir in the quinoa and parsley, and season to taste with salt and pepper.

BROILING AND PEELING BELL PEPPERS

The papery skin on red and yellow bell peppers is the part that promotes indigestion, so it has to go. Preheat the broiler, and line a shallow pan with aluminum foil. Lop the top and bottom off each pepper and slice into quarters, cutting through the flesh only. Discard the seedy core, and trim off any white inner ribs. You now have 4 flat pieces per pepper. Broil, skin side up, until the skin blackens and blisters, 5 to 7 minutes. (Yellow peppers take less time than red ones.) Cover with foil and let steam for 10 minutes. Pull off the papery skin, which comes off easily when you don't have to contend with curved ends.

Quinoa: The Inca Supergrain ⠒

One of the highest sources of protein in the vegetable kingdom, quinoa (pronounced *keen-wah*) has been cultivated in the Andean mountains for at least five thousand years. Reverently known as the "mother grain" to the Inca, Aztec, and other pre-Columbian peoples, for whom it had great religious significance, it's said that tireless Inca relay runners—who kept lines of communication open throughout the vast Inca empire—owed their legendary stamina to quinoa. It seems reasonable to suppose that this grain would be just as useful for the rest of us, even if we don't have to run up and down the snow-capped Andes.

Although treated as a grain, gluten-free quinoa is actually the fruit of a hardy plant belonging to the same family as beets, chard, and spinach, which can flourish at high altitudes. Chenopodium quinoa produces huge quantities of tiny but highly nutritious round seeds in large, sorghumlike clusters. When cooked, the grains swell and turn translucent, and the white nutrient ring shows clearly. High in minerals, quinoa supplies all the essential amino acids, making it a complete protein. It has a mellow, slightly nutty flavor, can be used like white rice, and cooks in only 15 minutes.

In addition to being available whole, organically grown American quinoa can be found in flakes, like rolled oats; as flour; and as pasta. The flakes are outstanding in muesli (page 25) and make an excellent binder for meat loaf or stuffings. The flour is useful for making breads and muffins. Available in natural foods stores, by mail order, and, increasingly, in supermarkets, there is just one caveat: whole-grain quinoa must be well rinsed before cooking to remove the naturally occurring, bitter-tasting saponins that form on the surface to repel insects.

quinoa salad with cucumber, tomato, and mint

BULGUR WHEAT, WHILE THE traditional grain for tabbouleh, is off-limits to those who can't eat wheat. Quinoa is the perfect substitute for bulgur. This "tabbouleh" keeps for two or three days refrigerated, and the grains do not harden when chilled. To make a complete summer meal, add cooked shrimp.

1. Bring the broth to a boil over high heat. Add the quinoa, reduce the heat to low, cover, and simmer until the grains are tender and the liquid is absorbed, about 15 minutes. The grains will turn transparent, and the white germ ring will show. Transfer to a large bowl and let cool.

2. Add the cucumber, tomatoes, green onions, radishes, mint, and parsley. Whisk together the olive oil and vinegar, and season to taste with salt and pepper. Pour over the quinoa and vegetables, and mix gently but thoroughly. Taste for seasoning and adjust as needed. Serve at room temperature.

2 cups gluten-free vegetable broth

1 cup red or yellow quinoa, rinsed and drained

1 cucumber (about 8 ounces), peeled, seeded, and chopped

2 large, ripe tomatoes, finely chopped, preferably heirloom

4 green onions, thinly sliced

8 radishes, finely chopped

1/4 cup chopped mint

1/2 cup chopped parsley

1/2 cup extra virgin olive oil

2 tablespoons wine vinegar

Fine sea salt and freshly ground black pepper

:: Serves 4 to 6

millet, mushroom, and bacon risotto

2 tablespoons extra
    virgin olive oil
1 onion, finely chopped
1 celery rib, destringed
    and finely chopped
½ pound white or brown
    mushrooms, sliced
1 cup millet
2½ cups gluten-free beef
    broth
8 strips lean bacon,
    cooked until crisp and
    crumbled
2 tablespoons chopped
    parsley
Fine sea salt and freshly
    ground black pepper

:: **Serves 2 as a main course;
    4 as a side dish**

THE ANCIENT ROMANS COOKED millet long before the arrival of corn or rice. Nutritious, quick-cooking, and gluten-free, it has a nutty, gentle flavor and a texture much like that of rice when cooked. Millet can be found in natural foods stores.

1. Heat the olive oil over medium-low heat until it shimmers. Add the onion and celery, and cook until softened but not browned, 5 minutes. Add the mushrooms, and cook until they lose their raw look, 2 minutes more. Stir in the millet, coating the grains well. Add the beef broth. Bring to a boil, reduce the heat to low, cover the pan, and simmer until the grains are tender but not mushy, 15 to 20 minutes.

2. Stir the bacon and parsley into the millet, and taste for seasoning, adding salt and pepper as needed.

millet pilaf with currants and hazelnuts

REVERED AS ONE OF the Five Sacred Grains in ancient China, millet is a mellow-tasting, healthful whole grain that's almost unknown in the United States except as birdseed. It can be used just like rice as a side dish, and makes an excellent addition to hearty soups.

1. Toast the hazelnuts lightly in a dry skillet, and set aside.

2. Heat the butter in the same skillet, add the onion, and cook until translucent and starting to turn color, about 7 minutes. Add the millet, stirring to coat the grains well. Season with ½ teaspoon salt and a generous grinding of black pepper. Add the chicken broth, ¾ cup water, and the currants. Bring to a boil, cover, reduce the heat to low, and simmer until tender, 15 to 20 minutes. Fluff with a fork, and stir in the hazelnuts and parsley.

¼ cup chopped hazelnuts

2 tablespoons unsalted butter

1 onion, finely chopped

1 cup millet

½ teaspoon fine sea salt

Freshly ground black pepper

1½ cups gluten-free chicken broth

¼ cup dried Zante currants

2 tablespoons chopped parsley

:: **Serves 4 to 6**

risotto with scallops

4 cups gluten-free
   chicken broth

2 tablespoons extra
   virgin olive oil

1 pound bay scallops
   (if using large sea
   scallops, cut in
   quarters)

Fine sea salt

6 tablespoons (¾
   stick) unsalted butter,
   softened

1 onion, finely chopped

1 garlic clove, minced

Pinch of dried red
   pepper flakes

2 cups Arborio rice

½ cup dry white wine

½ cup peeled, seeded,
   and chopped ripe
   tomato

¼ cup chopped parsley

∷ Serves 4 to 6

ONE OF THE GLORIES of northern Italian cuisine, risotto is really best made at home, not in a restaurant. It takes only about 25 minutes to cook, a soothing ritual that involves slowly adding broth to simmering Arborio rice, preferably sipping the same wine—maybe a Pinot Grigio delle Venezie—that goes into the dish. Round-grain Arborio, Carnaroli, or Vialone Nano rice is a must, as these highly similar varieties absorb broth without losing their shape and turn beautifully creamy. Long-grain white rice, which has a different starch content, would fall apart if cooked this way.

1. Blend the chicken broth with 2 cups water and bring to a simmer, then reduce the heat to very low so it doesn't evaporate.

2. Heat the olive oil in a large, heavy-bottomed saucepan over medium heat. Add the scallops. Sauté until the scallops become opaque, 2 minutes. Using a slotted spoon, transfer them to a plate and season lightly with salt, remembering that the broth may be salted.

3. Add 4 tablespoons of the butter to the pan. When hot and bubbling, add the onion and cook over medium-low heat until softened, 5 minutes. Add the garlic and red pepper flakes, and cook for 30 seconds. Stir in the rice with a wooden spoon. Add the wine, and when it has evaporated, stir in the tomato and ½ cup of the hot broth. Adding broth by the ¼ cupful as the rice absorbs the previous batch, continue cooking until the rice is creamy but still slightly firm to the bite, about 25 minutes. (If the broth gets used up before the rice is ready, add hot water.) The rice should not be allowed to become dry during cooking, but it should not be awash in liquid, either. The finished dish should look slightly soupy.

4. Taste-test frequently: when it is ready, a rice grain should just resist the bite and no more. Just before it's done, stir the scallops and parsley into the rice, and heat for 1 minute. Taste for seasoning, and stir in the remaining 2 tablespoons butter. Serve in warmed plates, using wide-rimmed soup plates, if available.

risotto with chicken livers

4 cups gluten-free
   chicken broth
4 tablespoons (½ stick)
   unsalted butter
1 onion, finely chopped
2 cups Arborio rice
Fine sea salt
½ cup dry white wine
2 tablespoons extra
   virgin olive oil
2 ounces pancetta, diced
2 portobello
   mushrooms, about
   4 ounces each, stem
   and brown underside
   removed, cut in
   ½-inch dice
¾ pound chicken livers,
   preferably free range,
   trimmed and cut in
   ½-inch dice
Freshly ground black
   pepper
½ cup chopped parsley

:: **Serves 4 to 6**

INEXPENSIVE CHICKEN LIVERS LEND richness to this flavorful risotto. To prevent the portobello mushrooms from staining the rice brown, remove the dark brown gills under the caps.

1. Blend the chicken broth with 2 cups water and bring to a simmer, then reduce the heat to very low so it doesn't evaporate.

2. Melt the butter in a large, heavy-bottomed saucepan over medium-low heat. Add half the chopped onion, and cook until softened, 5 minutes. Add the rice, and stir with a wooden spoon until it starts to turn translucent, 2 minutes. Season with salt if the broth is unsalted. Add the wine, and let it evaporate. Stir in the hot chicken broth, ¼ cup at a time, and continue cooking until the rice is creamy but still slightly firm to the bite, about 25 minutes. (If the broth gets used up before the rice is ready, add hot water.) The rice should not be allowed to get dry during cooking, but it should not be awash in liquid, either.

3. Fifteen minutes before the rice is done, heat the olive oil in a large skillet over medium heat. Add the remaining chopped onion and the pancetta, and sauté until the onion is softened, 5 minutes. Add the mushrooms, and sauté until the mushrooms are cooked through and look glassy, about 5 minutes. Push the onion-mushroom mixture to the edges of the pan, and add the chicken livers. Sauté until just done but still slightly pink inside, 1 to 2 minutes. (Do not overcook.) Season with salt and pepper. Mix with the onions and mushrooms, and remove from the heat. Sprinkle with the parsley. Gently fold the chicken-liver mixture into the rice, and serve on warmed plates, using wide-rimmed soup plates, if available.

grape leaf rolls with rice, currants, and pine nuts

40 grape leaves,
  preserved in brine
5 tablespoons extra
  virgin olive oil
1 medium onion, finely
  chopped
½ cup long-grain white
  rice
¼ teaspoon ground
  cinnamon
Fine sea salt
1 tablespoon chopped
  mint
2 tablespoons pine nuts
2 tablespoons dried
  Zante currants
Freshly ground black
  pepper
Juice of 1 lemon
Lemon wedges
Plain whole milk yogurt

:: **Makes about 30;
    serves 6 to 8**

A TENDER, FLAVORFUL SURPRISE, homemade stuffed grape vine leaves are nothing like the stodgy canned variety. A quart jar of grape leaves contains two rolled-up wads of about 40 leaves each; freeze one wad, enclosed in plastic wrap, to use another day.

1. Separate the grape leaves gently, rinse well, and blanch in boiling water for 3 minutes to soften. Plunge into cold water, and drain again. Lay 28 to 30 perfect leaves on a work surface, shiny side down, reserving any extra-large, extra-small, or torn ones. Nip off the stems.

2. In a heavy 10½-inch sauté pan with a lid, heat 2 tablespoons of the olive oil over medium heat until it shimmers. Add the onion, and sauté until golden, about 7 minutes. Add the rice and cinnamon, and turn to coat well. Add ½ teaspoon salt and 1 cup water, and bring to a boil. Cover, reduce the heat, and simmer for 5 minutes. Turn off the heat, and let stand until the rice is plumped up, about 15 minutes. Stir in the mint, pine nuts, currants, and a generous grinding of black pepper. Taste for seasoning, and add salt if

needed. Transfer the rice to a bowl, removing every last grain from the pan. Cover the bottom of the pan with a layer of reserved leaves, and drizzle with 1 tablespoon olive oil.

3. To make the rolls, center a tablespoon of filling on each leaf, fold the sides toward the center, and roll up to make a firm bundle. Place, seam side down, in the sauté pan, close together, in a single layer. Drizzle with the remaining 2 tablespoons olive oil and cover with a layer of leaves. Add the lemon juice and just enough water to cover. Weigh down with a heavy, heatproof plate, and cover the pan tightly. Cook over high heat for 5 minutes, then reduce the heat to low and simmer for 45 minutes. Let cool in the cooking liquid, most of which will have evaporated. Remove the rolls carefully with a slotted spatula. Serve at room temperature, with lemon wedges for squeezing on top and yogurt for dipping.

rice pilaf with fennel

2 tablespoons extra
  virgin olive oil
1 onion, finely chopped
2 fennel bulbs, 8 ounces
  each, trimmed,
  quartered, and sliced,
  green fronds reserved
  and chopped to make
  2 tablespoons
2 cups gluten-free
  chicken broth, heated
1 cup long-grain white
  rice
¼ cup minced fresh dill
  or 1 teaspoon dried
  dill
4 tablespoons unsalted
  butter, melted and
  lightly browned
Fine sea salt and freshly
  ground black pepper
Lemon wedges

:: Serves 2 as a main course;
   4 as a side dish

THIS APPETIZING, BUTTERY COMBI-NATION works as a vegetarian main course, an appetizer, or a side dish that's especially good with lamb.

1. Heat the olive oil over medium heat in a heavy saucepan. Add the onion, and cook until softened and starting to turn golden, 5 to 6 minutes. Add the fennel and ½ cup of the chicken broth and cook until softened, 10 minutes. Add the rice and dill, stirring well to coat the grains.
2. Add the remaining hot chicken stock. Cover, reduce the heat to low, and simmer until the rice and fennel are tender, 18 to 20 minutes.
3. Fluff the rice with a fork, and drizzle the browned butter on top. Toss gently to mix. Taste, and season with salt and pepper as needed—the chicken broth will probably contain salt. Spoon onto heated plates, and garnish with the chopped fennel fronds and the lemon wedges.

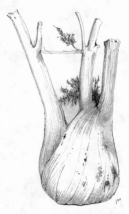

paella, la mancha style

THIS REGIONAL, INLAND VARIETY of paella makes an intriguing change from the more familiar Barcelona version with chicken and sea-food. Be sure to use round-grain Spanish or Italian rice here; long-grain white rice turns to mush. The sliced tomatoes on top give it a finished look as well as a fresh taste, and the golden fried potatoes, perhaps surprisingly, add great texture and flavor. Old Spanish recipes start with about half a pound of fresh lard; I use olive oil instead. An inexpensive, two-handled, 16-cup aluminum paella pan about 14 inches across adds to the presentation (and makes a useful all-purpose roasting pan), but dividing the ingredients between two large skillets also works.

1. Preheat the oven to 425°F. Heat 2 tablespoons of the olive oil in a 14-inch paella pan over medium-high heat until it shimmers. Add the potatoes, and fry until golden on both sides, about 10 minutes, and set aside.

2. Add the ham, garlic, sausages, and chorizo to the pan, and fry until the sausage slices are lightly colored, stirring constantly, 5 minutes. Stir in the rice. Add the chicken broth, saffron mixture, tomatoes, and potato slices. Season to taste with a little salt, remembering that the ham and broth will contain salt. Cover with

¼ cup extra virgin olive oil

1 pound small russet potatoes, peeled and sliced ¼ inch thick and patted dry on paper towels

¾ pound thickly sliced ham, diced

1 head of garlic, separated into cloves, peeled and sliced

4 best-quality, gluten-free pork sausages, sliced

2 ounces imported Spanish chorizo (cured sausage), diced

2½ cups Spanish paella rice or Arborio rice

5 cups gluten-free chicken broth, heated

Pinch of saffron threads, steeped in ¼ cup boiling water

1 cup peeled and diced tomatoes, drained (canned are fine)

Fine sea salt
Freshly ground black
    pepper to taste
2 large, ripe tomatoes,
    thickly sliced,
    preferably heirloom
Chopped parsley

∴ Serves 6 to 8

aluminum foil, and bake for 20 to 25 minutes until the rice is tender and almost dry. Meanwhile, heat the remaining 2 tablespoons olive oil in a large skillet. Fry the tomato slices on both sides until softened, 5 to 6 minutes, and season with salt and pepper. When the rice is cooked, garnish the surface with tomato slices and chopped parsley, and serve from the pan.

Pasta

ITALIAN PASTA HAS BECOME a favorite dish all over the world. Fortunately for the gluten-intolerant, quite a few of the classic dried forms, including spaghetti, fettuccine, spirals, shells, elbows, and lasagne, are now made from brown rice flour, corn, or quinoa. They are all mellow in flavor and cook in about the same length of time as wheat pasta. Different brands have slightly different textures, so keep trying until you find a favorite; I like both De Boles and Mrs. Leeper's pasta. You can also make your own fresh egg pasta from rice flour, which cooks in just 2 or 3 minutes. Traditional Asian rice noodles and mung bean noodles, which are marvelous for absorbing flavorful sauces, are gluten-free, cook in a flash, and can be found in many large supermarkets. At Asian groceries, the same item will cost far less.

rice spaghetti alla carbonara

PASTA CARBONARA IS TRADITIONALLY served with a sauce of pancetta and raw eggs, which are cooked, more or less, by the heat of the pasta. I don't fancy the idea of salmonella poisoning, so I use Eggbeaters instead. Made from 99 percent egg whites, this product is sterilized and perfectly safe. Again, it's not traditional, but the food police won't take you away if you add a handful of frozen peas to the boiling pasta water. Their sweetness makes the perfect foil for the pancetta and Parmesan.

5 to 6 ounces brown rice flour spaghetti
1 teaspoon fine sea salt
¼ cup frozen peas, optional
1 tablespoon extra virgin olive oil
3 ounces pancetta, diced
½ cup Eggbeaters or similar liquid egg substitute, at room temperature
Freshly ground black pepper
½ cup grated Parmigiano-Reggiano

:: **Serves 2**

1. Bring a pot of water to a boil, and add the salt and pasta. Cook until al dente, about 10 minutes, and drain. (Different manufacturers' products and instructions vary, so check frequently by biting into a strand.) If adding peas, do so a couple of minutes before the pasta is ready.
2. Meanwhile, heat the olive oil in a small skillet over medium-low heat. Add the pancetta, and sauté until lightly browned but not crisp, about 3 minutes. Set aside, still in the skillet. Season the Eggbeaters with black pepper, and stir in the Parmesan.
3. Drain the pasta, and add to the skillet with the pancetta. Pour the Eggbeater-Parmesan mixture on top, and toss to blend. The combined heat from the still-warm skillet and the hot pasta will cook it lightly. Divide between warmed plates.

rice fettuccine with arugula and goat cheese

5 to 6 ounces brown rice flour fettuccine

Fine sea salt and freshly ground black pepper

1 tablespoon extra virgin olive oil

1 tablespoon unsalted butter

2 medium onions, quartered and thinly sliced

2 cups (3 ounces) arugula

3 to 4 ounces soft white goat cheese, at room temperature

:: Serves 2

THIS RECIPE IS FAST, SAVORY, SIMPLE, and is easy to double. You can substitute coarsely chopped spinach for the arugula if you like.

1. Bring a pot of water to a boil and add a teaspoon of salt and the pasta. Cook until al dente, about 10 minutes, and drain. (Different manufacturers' products and instructions vary, so check frequently by biting into a strand.)

2. Meanwhile, heat the olive oil and butter in a skillet over medium-low heat. (The oil keeps the butter from scorching.) Add the onions and cook, stirring often, until soft and golden but not brown, 8 to 10 minutes. Add the arugula, and stir until wilted, 1 to 2 minutes. Season lightly with salt and pepper.

3. Add the pasta to the onion mixture, and toss. Divide between 2 warmed plates and crumble half the goat cheese over each portion. Add a generous grinding of pepper.

rice spirals with asparagus

THIS IS A PERFECT DISH FOR SPRING, when local asparagus starts appearing in the markets or your garden, should you be so lucky. Cook the asparagus until tender; it should be about the same consistency as the cooked pasta.

1. Bring a large pot of water to a rapid boil, and add the asparagus and a teaspoon of salt. Reduce the heat to medium, and simmer the asparagus until tender, about 5 minutes. Remove with tongs to a cutting board. Increase the heat to high, add the lemon zest and pasta spirals, and boil until the pasta is al dente, about 10 minutes. (Test often to check for doneness.) Cut the asparagus diagonally into 2-inch lengths.

2. Meanwhile, heat 2 tablespoons of the olive oil in a skillet over medium-low heat until it shimmers. Add the onion and red pepper flakes, and sauté until the onion is tender but not colored, about 5 minutes. Stir in the cut asparagus, heat gently, and season lightly with salt. Remove from the heat.

3. Drain the pasta and lemon zest, and add to the skillet. Add the remaining tablespoon olive oil, and toss gently to blend. Divide between warmed plates, and top with the Parmesan.

¾ pound slender asparagus, woody part of the stalks snapped off

Fine sea salt

4 strips lemon zest, 2 × ½ inch, slivered

5 to 6 ounces brown rice spirals

3 tablespoons extra virgin olive oil

1 small onion, chopped

Pinch of dried red pepper flakes

¼ cup grated Parmigiano-Reggiano

:: Serves 2

corn macaroni and cheese

4 tablespoons unsalted
  butter
3 tablespoons brown
  rice flour
2 cups milk, heated
Fine sea salt and freshly
  ground white pepper
Large pinch of nutmeg,
  preferably freshly
  grated
1 cup grated sharp
  Cheddar cheese
⅓ cup soft white Rice
  Flour Bread Crumbs
  (page 134)
8 ounces corn pasta
  elbows
2 tablespoons grated
  Parmigiano-Reggiano

:: Serves 4

MAC-AND-CHEESE IS A DISH that needs
to be homemade before it can become the stuff of
which fond memories are made. Rice or quinoa
pasta elbows work equally well.

1. Preheat the oven to 375°F. Bring a large pot of water to
a rolling boil. Grease a 6-cup shallow baking dish.

2. Melt 3 tablespoons of the butter in a heavy saucepan
over medium-low heat. Add the rice flour, and stir until
smooth, 20 seconds. Add the hot milk, and whisk until
the mixture boils and thickens, about 2 minutes. Season
to taste with salt, pepper, and the nutmeg. Stir in ¾ cup
of the grated Cheddar and set aside.

3. Melt the remaining tablespoon butter in a small skillet
over low heat, stir in the bread crumbs, and remove from
the heat.

4. Meanwhile, add 1 teaspoon salt and the corn elbows
to the boiling water. Stir to prevent clumping and cook
until al dente, 6 to 10 minutes depending on the brand
(test often), and drain. Add to the cheese sauce, and pour
into the baking dish. Sprinkle with the remaining grated
Cheddar and the Parmesan, and scatter the buttered
bread crumbs on top. Bake uncovered until the sauce
bubbles and the top is tinged golden brown, about 20
minutes. (If it's not brown enough by then, broil for 2
minutes.) Let cool for 10 minutes before serving.

gratinéed rice flour cannelloni

HERE, TENDER RICE CRÊPES are filled with a savory meat mixture but not blanketed with the usual flour-based béchamel or tomato sauce. The ragù recipe makes about 6 cups; freeze the remainder for serving with gluten-free pasta, mixed with ricotta, cooked spinach, or lightly cooked tomato to loosen it a bit. Time permitting, make the ragù a day ahead so that the flavors can develop.

1. To make the ragù: Heat the olive oil in a large, heavy-bottomed saucepan over medium-low heat. Add the onion, and sauté until softened, about 5 minutes. Add the beef, breaking it up well, and cook until it loses its pink color, about 10 minutes. Stir in the wine, and cook for 2 minutes more. Add the prosciutto, fennel seeds, tomatoes, and tomato paste. Bring to a boil, mashing the tomatoes with a wooden spoon. Reduce the heat, partially cover the pan, and simmer gently, stirring occasionally, until the mixture is reduced to approximately 6 cups, about 3 hours. Taste, and season with salt and pepper. Transfer to a bowl, let cool, cover, and refrigerate.

2. To assemble: Preheat the oven to 425°F. Grease a ceramic baking dish large enough to hold the cannelloni in one layer (or use two smaller ones) with 2 tablespoons of the butter. Blend the ragù with the ricotta, half the

RAGÙ

2 tablespoons extra virgin olive oil

1 onion, finely chopped

2 pounds ground beef

1 cup dry white wine

¼ pound prosciutto, with fat, chopped and processed to a paste

½ teaspoon fennel seeds

1 large can (28 ounces) Italian tomatoes, with their juice

2 tablespoons tomato paste

Fine sea salt and freshly ground black pepper

:: Serves 4 to 6

4 tablespoons unsalted
   butter
12 Rice Flour Crêpes
   (page 22)
2 cups Ragù
½ cup ricotta
½ cup freshly grated
   Parmigiano-Reggiano
3 tablespoons chopped
   parsley

Parmesan, and the parsley. Lay the crêpes on a work surface, browned side down. Place ⅓ cup filling down the center of each one and roll up, without tucking in the ends. Place the filled crêpes, seam side down, in the baking dish, touching each other. Dot with the remaining 2 tablespoons butter, and sprinkle with the remaining Parmesan. Bake until light golden brown and the ends of the rolled crêpes are crispy, about 15 minutes. Let rest for 10 minutes before serving.

fresh rice flour egg pasta

MAKING YOUR OWN PASTA will elicit awe and admiration (unless, of course, you have an Italian grandmother), but it's really easy using rice flour, as the pasta dough doesn't resist being rolled out. It can be cut into any width you like: 1/4 inch wide for fettuccine, 1/2 inch wide for pappardelle, or 2 inches wide for lasagne. The recipe makes two 12 × 10-inch sheets of silky pasta, weighing about 4 ounces each, and can be doubled. As with all fresh pasta, it cooks in just 2 or 3 minutes.

2/3 cup brown rice flour
1/3 cup tapioca flour
1/2 teaspoon xanthan gum
1/2 teaspoon fine sea salt
1 large egg
1 large egg yolk
1 tablespoon extra virgin olive oil

1. Combine the rice flour, tapioca flour, xanthan gum, and salt in a food processor, and process to mix. Combine the egg, egg yolk, olive oil, and 1 tablespoon water in a glass measuring cup, and whisk to combine. With the motor running, pour the egg mixture over the flour, and pulse until the dough forms into a rough ball. (If too dry, add a few drops of water; if too wet, add a little more rice flour.) Remove, and pat together into a disk. Cut the dough in half, and work with one half at a time.

2. Place a ball of dough between 2 sheets of plastic wrap and roll into a very thin, even rectangle approximately 10 × 12 inches, turning it several times. (Italian cooks say you should be able to read newspaper headlines through rolled pasta dough.). Repeat with the remaining dough.

:: **Makes 1/2 pound; serves 2**

If using immediately, peel off the top layer of plastic wrap and cut the dough into strips of desired width. (If refrigerating or freezing, leave the sheets inside the plastic wrap and cut later.) Peel the strips away from the bottom sheet of plastic wrap and lay on a wooden board, so you can add them to the boiling water all at once.

3. Bring 2 quarts water to a rolling boil. Add 1 teaspoon salt and the pasta. Cook, stirring occasionally, until the pasta is al dente, 2 to 3 minutes. Drain and toss with butter and Parmigiano-Reggiano, or your choice of sauce.

rice pappardelle with mushroom sauce

FRESHLY MADE WIDE NOODLES are uniquely satisfying to eat. Maybe it's their slurpiness. Pappardelle are usually served *con lepre*— with hare sauce—but you can serve this pasta with a rich and chunky mushroom sauce instead. Grated Parmesan would be superfluous here.

1. Cut the pasta into ½-inch wide strips and set aside.

2. Lift the porcini mushroom pieces from the soaking liquid, pat dry, and chop coarsely. Strain the liquid through a paper coffee filter into a small bowl, and reserve.

3. Heat the butter and olive oil in a skillet over medium-low heat. (The oil will prevent the butter from scorching.) Add the onion and garlic, and cook until softened but not browned, 5 minutes. Add the sliced mushrooms. Sprinkle with the thyme, and add salt and pepper to taste. Cook, stirring often, until the mushrooms turn glassy-looking, about 5 minutes. Add the reserved porcini soaking liquid, ¾ cup of the beef broth, and the Marsala. Reduce the heat to low, and simmer until the mushrooms and onion are tender, 10 to 15 minutes, adding the remaining beef broth if needed to make a fairly liquid sauce. Taste for seasoning.

8 ounces Fresh Rice Flour Egg Pasta (page 75)

½ ounce dried porcini mushrooms, soaked in 1 cup warm water for 20 minutes

3 tablespoons unsalted butter

1 tablespoon extra virgin olive oil

1 onion, finely chopped

2 garlic cloves, minced

2 ounces pancetta or lean bacon, finely chopped

¾ pound assorted mushrooms (white, cremini, hen-of-the-woods, morels, etc.), sliced

1 teaspoon dried thyme

Fine sea salt and freshly ground black pepper

1 cup gluten-free beef broth

2 tablespoons Marsala

2 teaspoons cornstarch,
   dissolved in 2
   tablespoons water

:: **Serves 4 as a first course**

4. Meanwhile, bring a large pot of water to a rolling boil; add 1 teaspoon salt and the pasta strips. Boil until al dente, 2 to 3 minutes, drain, and pour into a heated serving bowl.

5. Stir the cornstarch mixture, and add to the mushroom mixture. Let simmer until it thickens slightly and clears, 30 seconds or less. Pour over the pasta, and toss gently to mix.

asian stick noodles with pork and asparagus

NESTS OF BUNDLED AND dried Asian rice stick noodles can be found in many large supermarkets, along with condiments like bean sauce and oyster sauce, which are off-limits as they contain wheat. Here I've teamed stick noodles with pork with asparagus, but shrimp and snow peas or chicken breast with broccoli work well with the same seasoning sauce. As a wok doesn't get hot enough on a regular stovetop, I use a large sauté pan for better heat contact. Stir the sauce ingredients together first.

SEASONING SAUCE

2 tablespoons wheat-free tamari sauce, such as San-J Organic Tamari

2 tablespoons dry sherry

½ cup gluten-free chicken broth

1 teaspoon toasted sesame oil

½ teaspoon sugar

1 teaspoon fine sea salt

1. For the seasoning sauce: Combine the tamari sauce, sherry, chicken broth, sesame oil, sugar, and salt, and set aside.

2. Bring a large pot of water to a boil, add the noodles (do not soak first), and cook for 3 minutes, stirring occasionally to separate the strands. Pour into a colander, run cold water over the noodles, and reserve.

4 ounces Asian rice stick noodles

2 tablespoons peanut or corn oil

½ pound lean pork (boneless chops are fine), thinly sliced

½ teaspoon fine sea salt

1 garlic clove, minced

Pinch of dried red pepper flakes

4 green onions, most of
the tops included, cut
in 2-inch pieces and
slivered lengthways
½ pound pencil-thin
asparagus, woody
ends discarded, cut in
2-inch lengths

:: Serves 2

3. Heat a large sauté pan over medium-high heat. Add 1 tablespoon of the oil and tip the pan to spread it around. Add the pork, and stir-fry until it turns beige and is barely cooked through, 2 minutes. Transfer to a plate and sprinkle with the salt.

4. Add the remaining tablespoon oil to the pan, swirl it around, and add the garlic, red pepper flakes, and green onions. Let cook for 20 seconds, then add the asparagus. Stir-fry for 1 minute, add 2 or 3 tablespoons water to create steam, and continue stir-frying until tender-crisp, about 3 minutes. Add the noodles, and toss well. Add the seasoning sauce, and allow it to evaporate, tossing the mixture constantly, about 2 minutes more. Return the pork and any juices to the pan, and heat through, stirring and tossing, for 1 minute. Serve immediately.

buckwheat spaetzle

FUN TO MAKE, THESE tiny dumplings can be served as a side dish with braised meat or chicken, or eaten like pasta with the addition of grated Parmigiano-Reggiano. If you don't have a spaetzle press, which looks a bit like a flat grater with a movable carriage that slides back and forth, use a colander with 1/4-inch wide holes and a rubber spatula instead. For a different flavor, replace the buckwheat flour with chestnut or teff flour.

1/4 cup buckwheat flour
1/2 cup brown rice flour
1/4 cup cornstarch
Fine sea salt
1/4 teaspoon nutmeg, preferably freshly grated
2 large eggs, lightly beaten
3 to 4 tablespoons milk
1 tablespoon canola oil
3 tablespoons unsalted butter, softened
Freshly ground black pepper

:: Serves 4

1. Sift the buckwheat flour, rice flour, cornstarch, 1/4 teaspoon salt, and the nutmeg into a bowl. Using a fork, stir in the eggs and 3 tablespoons of the milk to make a lumpy-looking batter. Keep stirring, and add the remaining tablespoon milk if needed. The dough should not be runny: if you lift the fork, it should hang for a moment before dropping.

2. Bring a large pot of water to a boil over medium-high heat. Add 1 tablespoon salt and the canola oil, which helps to prevent clumping. Grease a serving dish with 1 tablespoon of the butter, and keep warm.

3. Rest a spaetzle press over the pot, and spoon 1/2 cup of the batter into the movable carriage. Slide this back and forth, which will push little curls of dough into the water. The spaetzle will swell and rise to the surface almost immediately. Let cook for 1 minute, and remove with

a slotted spoon to a heated serving dish. Repeat with the remaining batter. Add the remaining 2 tablespoons butter to the dish, season to taste with salt and pepper, and toss well. (Alternatively, toss the spaetzle with a little vegetable oil, so they don't stick together, and let cool. Heat in butter just before serving.)

Birds

ANYONE WHO IS GLUTEN-SENSITIVE WILL be delighted to discover that chicken does not have to be limited to the plain roasted kind. A delicious breading mixture made from ground nuts and Parmesan adds new savor to sautéed breast meat, and whole birds can be flattened and then plumped under the skin with a tasty mushroom stuffing. The holiday bird benefits from a new, meatier, gluten-free dressing, and the accompanying gravy is just as good when thickened with rice flour or cornstarch and livened up with Spanish sherry.

hazelnut and parmesan chicken cutlets

WORLDS AWAY FROM DEEP-FRIED fast food, slices of tender chicken breast have a light, crispy coating that's full of flavor. The recipe can, of course, be doubled; but use two pans or the cutlets will steam instead of brown. They should not touch each other as they cook. If you can't find hazelnut meal, make it yourself by grinding hazelnuts in an electric coffee mill reserved for grinding spices and other items; a food processor tends to make nut paste rather than flour.

1. Remove the long fillet and slice the chicken meat horizontally (see below), making 4 slices. Combine the hazelnut meal and Parmesan on a plate. Beat the egg in a shallow bowl, and season with salt and pepper,

2. Heat the olive oil in a skillet over medium heat until it shimmers. Dip the chicken pieces in the rice flour, shaking off any excess, then in the seasoned egg, and finally in the cheese-hazelnut blend. Sauté until golden brown on both sides and cooked through, 3 minutes or less. Place on heated dinner plates, drizzle with hazelnut oil, if using, and garnish with lemon wedges.

SLICING CHICKEN BREASTS HORIZONTALLY

A chicken breast is an awkward shape for even cooking, so many recipes recommend beating it flat. Slicing the

2 chicken breast halves,
  6 ounces each,
  skinless and boneless
3/4 cup hazelnut meal
1/4 cup grated
  Parmigiano-Reggiano
1 large egg
Fine sea salt and freshly
  ground white pepper
2 tablespoons extra
  virgin olive oil
White rice flour, for
  dredging
Hazelnut oil, optional
Lemon wedges

:: Serves 2

meat horizontally is quicker, gives a better texture, and impresses onlookers no end. Wielding a sharp paring knife, locate and remove the partially detached long fillet from a skinned and boned chicken breast half and set aside. (Either cook the fillet alongside the breast meat, or freeze for a stir-fry another day.) Place the breast meat on a wooden chopping board, with the rounded, skin side uppermost. Lay one hand flat on top, fingers outstretched. Slice the breast into equal halves or thirds (depending on size and thickness) with a sawing motion, parallel to the board and safely underneath your palm.

chicken in chardonnay

INSPIRED BY A THRIFTY French country recipe for turning a tough old cockerel into something worthwhile, this lighter version of coq au vin substitutes the succulent thigh meat of young chickens and white wine for an old bird and red wine, the sauce is thickened with a little cornstarch, and it takes far less time to cook. Serve with quinoa or long-grain white rice.

2 pounds boneless, skinless chicken thighs
Fine sea salt and freshly ground black pepper
2 tablespoons extra virgin olive oil
1 tablespoon unsalted butter
¼ cup brandy
1 onion, chopped
2 garlic cloves, chopped
1 cup Chardonnay
1 to 1½ cups gluten-free chicken broth
2 bay leaves
3 strips lean bacon, diced
8 ounces shallots, peeled and separated along natural divisions
12 medium white or brown mushrooms (about ¾ pound), halved
1 tablespoon cornstarch
¼ cup chopped parsley

1. Remove any loose fat from the chicken thighs, and cut in half lengthways. Season with salt and pepper.

2. Heat half the olive oil and the butter in a large sauté pan over medium heat. Brown the chicken pieces on both sides, about 7 minutes, in two batches if necessary. Remove the pan from the heat. Pour the brandy over the chicken, avert your face, and carefully ignite. When the flames die down, transfer the chicken and any juices to a bowl.

3. Return the pan to medium heat, and add the remaining olive oil. Stir in the onion and cook until translucent, about 5 minutes. Stir in the garlic. Add the wine, scraping with a wooden spoon to

:: **Serves 6**

bring up all the browned bits from the bottom of the pan, and bring to a boil. Add the bay leaves. Return the chicken and accumulated juices to the pan, add ½ cup of the chicken broth, and bring to a simmer. Reduce the heat to low, cover, and simmer for 15 minutes. Turn the chicken pieces, adding more chicken stock if necessary to prevent drying out, and continue simmering until the chicken is tender and the juices run clear if pierced with a knife tip, another 15 minutes.

4. Meanwhile, heat a large skillet over medium-low heat and add the bacon. When the fat starts to run, 2 to 3 minutes, add the shallots and mushrooms. Sauté until lightly colored, 5 minutes, then add ½ cup chicken broth and bring to a boil. Reduce the heat to low, cover the pan, and simmer until tender, 10 to 15 minutes, depending on the size of the shallots.

5. When ready to serve, add the shallots and mushrooms to the chicken. Mix the cornstarch with 1 tablespoon water, stir into the sauce, and let bubble until it thickens and clears, 30 seconds or less. Transfer to a heated serving dish, discarding the bay leaves, and sprinkle with the parsley.

ground chicken roll with quinoa

THIS UPSCALE VERSION OF meat loaf becomes a pâté when cold, and will keep refrigerated for three days. Serve hot with a marinara sauce, or cold with salad greens. The secret ingredient—quinoa flakes—promotes a smooth texture, and paper-thin zucchini slices, rather than fat, keep it moist. Vacuum-packed prosciutto is the best choice here, as the slices are large and uniform and are separated by paper sheets for easy handling.

1. Heat the oven to 350°F. Lay a large sheet of aluminum foil on a work surface, and lightly grease an 8 × 8-inch area in the center with olive oil.

2. Crack the egg into a mixing bowl, and beat lightly. Stir in the orange zest, zucchini, quinoa, salt, pepper, fennel seeds, and pistachios, if using. Add the ground chicken and mix gently but thoroughly. Lay 3 or 4 slices of the prosciutto on the foil, slightly overlapping, to form a 6 × 8-inch rectangle. Mound the chicken mixture along the center at a right angle to the slices, forming a roll. Bring the prosciutto up around both sides. Lay another slice of prosciutto lengthwise along the top and pat into place; it will cling to the roll. Turn the roll over so that the striped surface is on top, and brush lightly with olive oil. Using the foil as a sling, transfer the roll and foil to a

Extra virgin olive oil

1 large egg

2 teaspoons minced orange zest

1 medium zucchini, very thinly sliced

¼ cup quinoa flakes

1 teaspoon fine sea salt

Freshly ground black pepper

¼ teaspoon fennel seeds, crushed

¼ cup dry-roasted, unsalted pistachios, optional

1 pound boneless, skinless chicken leg meat, coarsely ground (see page 90)

4 to 5 large slices (about 3 ounces) prosciutto

∷ **Serves 4**

shallow roasting pan. Bake, uncovered, until just cooked through and a meat thermometer inserted near the center registers 165°F, about 50 minutes. Let the chicken roll cool for 10 minutes before slicing.

GROUND CHICKEN

Buy ready-ground chicken meat only from a reliable market with a high turnover. Given half a chance, bacteria rejoice and multiply on the many surfaces of ground raw poultry, or any meat for that matter, that's left sitting around. Alternatively, grind chicken yourself in a food processor. *With the motor running,* drop boneless and skinless chunks through the feed tube, stopping when the meat is coarsely ground. Don't overdo it, or you'll end up with a paste.

chicken and quinoa moroccan style

IN THIS VARIATION ON NORTH African couscous, a savory dish of semolina grains steamed over a savory chicken or lamb and vegetable stew, quinoa replaces the wheat couscous. The traditional accompaniment for couscous is an incendiary condiment called harissa. Make it first.

1. Season the chicken with salt and pepper. Heat 2 tablespoons of the olive oil in a 10- or 12-inch sauté pan over medium-high heat until it shimmers. Add the chicken, and sauté until browned on the outside but still slightly pink in the center (cut to test), about 4 minutes. Set aside on a plate.

2. Add the remaining tablespoon olive oil to the pan. Add the onion and garlic, and cook, stirring often, until softened, about 5 minutes. Add the ginger, cumin, saffron, and red pepper flakes, and cook until fragrant, 30 seconds. Add the carrots, bell pepper, tomatoes, and chicken broth. Reduce the heat to low. Simmer, uncovered, until the vegetables are tender-crisp, about 10 minutes. Stir in the zucchini, and continue cooking until tender, about 10 minutes longer. Taste and adjust the seasoning with salt and pepper. Return the chicken to the pan, and gently reheat.

3. To make the garnish: Ten minutes before the chicken is ready, heat the olive oil in a skillet over medium heat.

1 pound boned and skinned chicken breast meat, cut into 1-inch chunks

Fine sea salt and freshly ground black pepper

3 tablespoons extra virgin olive oil

1 onion, chopped

1 garlic clove, minced

1 teaspoon ground ginger

1 teaspoon ground cumin

Generous pinch of saffron threads or 1/4 teaspoon ground turmeric

1/8 teaspoon dried red pepper flakes

2 cups baby carrots

1 red bell pepper, ribs and seeds removed, cut into 1-inch chunks

2 ripe tomatoes, cored and cut into 1-inch chunks

1½ cups gluten-free
chicken broth
2 zucchini, quartered
lengthwise and cut
into 1-inch chunks

GARNISH
1 tablespoon extra virgin
olive oil
¼ cup chopped walnuts
or pine nuts
½ cup raisins, soaked
in hot water for 10
minutes, drained
½ cup lightly packed
fresh cilantro leaves,
stems discarded

Harissa Sauce (recipe
follows)
Quinoa (recipe follows)

:: **Serves 4**

Add the walnuts, and brown lightly, 2 minutes. Stir in the raisins, and remove from the heat.

4. To serve, mound the quinoa onto a warmed platter or 4 warmed dinner plates. Spoon the chicken, vegetables, and broth over the quinoa. Garnish with the walnuts, raisins, and cilantro. Pass the harissa at the table. Serves 4.

harissa sauce

Combine 2 to 3 tablespoons red pepper flakes, 4 teaspoons caraway seeds, 2 teaspoons cumin seeds, and 1 teaspoon salt in a spice grinder or clean electric coffee mill, and grind to a coarse powder. Mash 4 chopped garlic cloves to a paste. In a small saucepan, combine the garlic paste with the ground spices and ⅓ cup extra virgin olive oil. Simmer very gently for 5 minutes. Let cool. Makes about ½ cup. Serve in a small bowl.

quinoa

1 cup light yellow quinoa
2 cups gluten-free
   chicken broth or water
Salt, optional

A half hour before it is needed, rinse the quinoa to wash off any naturally occurring bitter saponins. Bring the broth to a boil over high heat. Add the quinoa and salt, if needed (the broth may be salty enough; if using water, add ½ teaspoon salt), reduce the heat to low, cover the pan, and simmer until the grains are tender and the liquid is absorbed, about 15 minutes.

chicken with mushroom stuffing

3½- to 4-pound chicken, skin intact

STUFFING

1 ounce dried porcini mushrooms, soaked in warm water for 20 minutes

¼ cup quinoa flakes

5 tablespoons unsalted butter, softened

1 tablespoon extra virgin olive oil

1 small onion, minced

2 garlic cloves, minced

1 portobello mushroom, about 4 ounces, finely chopped

2 ounces prosciutto, finely chopped

2 teaspoons chopped fresh thyme or 1 teaspoon dried thyme

Fine sea salt and freshly ground black pepper

WEALTHY ANCIENT ROMANS FATTENED chickens on bread soaked in wine and hydromel, a kind of liquor made with fermented honey. The birds gorged themselves silly, attained an enormous weight, and were reputed to taste exquisite. Not having any chickens or mead with which to practice, I can't vouch for the Roman method, but I can recommend enhancing a regular chicken's size and flavor by stuffing it under the skin. To make the savory stuffing, you will need bread crumbs made from day-old Quick White Rice Flour Flatbread (page 133).

1. Remove any excess fat and the giblets from the chicken, rinse, and pat dry. Using poultry shears or a sharp knife, cut along either side of the backbone, through the ribs, and discard it. Open the bird out and give it a firm blow or two, using the heel of your hand, to flatten the breast further.

2. To make the stuffing: Lift the porcini pieces from the bowl, reserving the aromatic soaking liquid for another use, squeeze dry, and chop finely.

3. Heat 4 tablespoons of the butter and the olive oil (which will

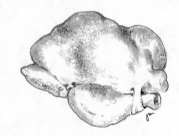

prevent it from scorching) in a large sauté pan over medium-low heat. Add the onion, garlic, portobello, porcini, and prosciutto. Sprinkle with the thyme, and season with salt and pepper. Simmer gently until softened, about 10 minutes. Stir in the bread crumbs and quinoa flakes, and remove from the heat. Let cool for 10 minutes, and stir in the egg.

4. Preheat the oven to 375°F.

5. Loosen the skin of the chicken from the flesh over the breast and legs with your fingers, being careful not to tear it, but don't detach at the sides. Insert small handfuls of stuffing under the skin, pushing it along from on top. Mold and plump the bird into its original shape. Make two 1-inch slits in the skin just short of the drumstick ends, toward the tail. Poke the drumsticks through the slits and fold the wing tips under, which helps to keep the chicken flat as it roasts. Smear with the remaining tablespoon butter and sprinkle with salt and pepper. Place on a rack in a roasting pan. Roast until golden brown and an instant-read meat thermometer inserted in the breast reaches 165°F, basting twice with the pan juices after the first half hour, about 40 minutes in all. Transfer to a warmed platter, and discard the fatty drippings. Let rest for 10 minutes, and cut into quarters.

½ cup soft white Rice Flour Bread Crumbs (page 134)
1 large egg, lightly beaten

∴ **Serves 4**

lemon-parsley chicken legs

4 whole chicken legs,
   6 to 8 ounces each
3 tablespoons unsalted
   butter
1 tablespoon extra virgin
   olive oil
1 small onion, finely
   chopped
4 tablespoons chopped
   parsley
Grated zest of 1 lemon
3/4 cup soft white Rice
   Flour Bread Crumbs
   (page 134)
Fine sea salt and freshly
   ground black pepper

:: **Serves 4**

STUFFING WHOLE CHICKEN LEGS under the skin with a mixture of onion, parsley, lemon, and rice flour bread crumbs makes them look and taste special, and they can be prepared several hours ahead of baking. A pilaf made with rice, millet, or quinoa goes well here.

1. Preheat the oven to 350°F. Line a shallow baking pan or a rimmed baking sheet with aluminum foil.

2. Separate the skin of the chicken legs from the flesh with your fingers, but don't detach at the sides. Cut through the skin around the joint, severing all the white tendons. Using a paper towel for a good grip, hold the tendons one at a time and pull; then cut out as much as possible. These tendons toughen even more when cooked, so removing them makes the drumstick meat more inviting.

3. Heat 2 tablespoons of the butter and the olive oil (which will prevent scorching) in a skillet over medium-low heat. Add the onion and cook gently until softened but not browned, about 7 minutes.
Stir in the parsley, lemon zest, and bread crumbs, and remove from the heat. Season with salt and pepper

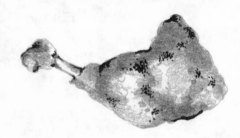

and let cool for 10 minutes. The stuffing will look dry.

4. Insert one-quarter of the stuffing under the skin of each chicken leg, like filling a bag, pushing it along from on top. Mold and plump the chicken legs back into their original shape. (The chicken can be refrigerated at this stage.) Place in the baking pan and smear them with the remaining tablespoon of butter. Season lightly with salt and pepper. Roast for 20 minutes, baste with the rendered fat, and continue roasting for another 20 minutes until the skin is brown and crispy and the juices run clear when pierced with a knife tip.

chicken with celery and tarragon

1¼ pounds chicken
  thigh meat, skinless
  and boneless
Fine sea salt and freshly
  ground white pepper
¼ cup white rice flour
2 tablespoons extra
  virgin olive oil
2 tablespoons diced
  pancetta
1 onion, diced
4 celery ribs, destringed
  and chopped
2 teaspoons chopped
  fresh tarragon or
  1 teaspoon dried
  tarragon
½ cup white wine
½ cup gluten-free
  chicken broth
Finely chopped celery
  leaves

:: **Serves 4**

AROMATIC FRENCH TARRAGON TURNS simple ingredients into an outstanding dish. Serve with Quick White Rice Flour Flatbread (page 133) or basmati rice for taking up the sauce.

1. Cut the chicken thighs in half lengthwise and season with salt and pepper. Just before cooking, dust with rice flour, shaking off the excess. (Do this at the last minute so they don't become gummy and inhibit the browning process.)

2. In a sauté pan, heat the olive oil over medium-low heat until it shimmers. Add the chicken pieces, and brown on both sides, about 5 minutes. Remove to a plate.

3. Add the pancetta, onion, celery, and tarragon, and cook until the vegetables are softened but not colored, about 5 minutes. Add the wine to the pan, scraping up any good browned bits, and let bubble for 2 minutes to reduce slightly. Stir in the chicken broth, and bring to a boil. Return the chicken to the pan, turning to coat well. Reduce the heat, cover, and simmer until the chicken is cooked through, turning once, about 15 minutes. Taste for seasoning. Divide the chicken among warmed plates. Spoon the sauce on top, and scatter with celery leaves.

chicken and chestnut soup

RATHER LIKE A CLASSIC game soup in taste and texture, this velvety chestnut soup contains chunks of juicy, just-cooked-through chicken rather than the more usual croutons. It makes a spectacular first course for a fall or winter dinner party. Canned chestnut purée is very dense, so it helps to chop it before adding to the soup.

1. In a large pot, melt 2 tablespoons of the butter over medium-low heat. Add the onion and celery and cook, stirring, until softened but not colored, 3 minutes. Stir in the Herbes de Provence Blend. Add the chicken broth and the chestnut purée, crushing it into the broth with a potato masher until smooth. Simmer, stirring occasionally, until the vegetables are tender, 20 minutes. The soup will thicken as it cooks; if it gets too thick, add a little water. Taste, and add salt and pepper as needed, remembering that the broth will probably contain salt.

2. Meanwhile, melt the remaining tablespoon butter in a skillet over medium heat. Add the chicken, and sauté until just cooked through, about 1 minute. Season lightly with salt and pepper, and add to the soup just before serving.

3. Ladle into warmed soup bowls. Float a tablespoon of sour cream on top of each serving, and scatter with chopped celery leaves.

3 tablespoons unsalted butter

1 small onion, finely chopped

2 celery ribs, destringed and finely chopped

2 teaspoons Herbes de Provence Blend (page 101), or 1 teaspoon dried store-bought blend

4 cups gluten-free chicken broth

1 (15½-ounce) can unsweetened chestnut purée, such as Clément Faugier

Fine sea salt and freshly ground black pepper

2 boneless and skinless chicken thighs (4 ounces each), well trimmed and cut in ½-inch cubes

6 tablespoons sour cream

Chopped celery leaves,
    from tops of small
    inner ribs

:: **Serves 6**

The only snag to using this aromatic vegetable is that the fibrous strings don't soften during cooking, which can make even diced celery unexpectedly chewy. Whip the tough strings off in seconds by running a vegetable peeler over the back of each rib before using.

herbes de provence blend

THIS CLASSIC HERB BLEND originated in southern France, where wild herbs grow in profusion on sunny hillsides. You can buy imported dried Herbes de Provence blends, but making your own fresh blend gives even more aromatic results. Dried lavender for culinary use is available at natural foods stores.

Using a mortar and pestle, pound the lavender until broken up. If you don't have a mortar, enclose the lavender in plastic wrap and pound with the base of a heavy saucepan. Blend with the minced rosemary, thyme, and marjoram. Store any extra in the freezer.

½ teaspoon dried lavender

2 teaspoons fresh rosemary leaves, minced

2 teaspoons fresh thyme leaves, minced

1 teaspoon fresh marjoram leaves, minced

:: Makes about 4 teaspoons

The Versatile Chestnut ::

Even though it's a nut, the fat content of the European chestnut is low, less than 3 percent, so when dried and ground, chestnuts make a useful flour. Years ago, poor Italian country dwellers with no access to wheat flour baked an unleavened chestnut flour flatbread on a hot hearthstone, rather like traditional Scottish oatcakes or Mexican tortillas. But when times got better, bread made from wheat took its place. Today, Italians bake a similar dense, low, unsweetened cake flavored with olive oil and rosemary, called castagnaccio, but use an oven rather than a hearthstone.

By contrast, candied chestnuts, chestnut pastries, and chestnut spread are luxury foods enjoyed all over Europe. Chestnut flour makes good cakes, pancakes, and spaetzle.

Although it's naturally sweet, the French favor chestnut purée with game such as wild boar and venison. Whole chestnuts go well with pork, chicken, and buttered baby Brussels sprouts, and in stuffing.

During the fall and winter months, stores in North America sell glossy fresh chestnuts in the shell for roasting over an open fire. Whole chestnuts dry out quickly, so it's better to seek out locally grown crops rather than imports, which will have been treated with fungicides. Go online and purchase directly from American growers, who sell excellent fresh chestnuts, dried chestnuts, and sweetly scented chestnut flour. (See page 211.) Depending on how old it is, imported chestnut flour can develop an unpleasant, strong scent and flavor. The only way to find out is to ask the store manager to open a bag for you.

Getting a chestnut out of its inner shell and removing the bitter interior skin requires patience. You can cut through the skin almost all the way around the nuts, like a belt, and roast a small batch at a time in a 400°F oven for a few minutes, then peel them before they have time to cool off. Or you can cut a cross into the flat side and microwave them, allowing 8 minutes for a pound of nuts, and then peel them, but this method won't give you that agreeable roasted flavor.

Alternatively, you can buy roasted, peeled, ready-to-use whole chestnuts in jars or plastic pouches at upscale grocery stores, where you can also find sweetened and unsweetened chestnut purée. Don't bother with canned European chestnuts in water. They have little flavor and fall apart at the least provocation. Incidentally, the crunchy white Chinese water chestnut commonly found in cans is not a nut at all but a corm, or bulb. You can't use them in place of European chestnuts.

roast capon with chestnut and sausage dressing

WE'RE ALL SO USED to eating very young chickens that the taste and texture of a properly raised mature one comes as a delicious surprise. A capon is simply a neutered chicken, fattened slowly until it reaches a majestic size and has developed some real flavor. You can order one from a butcher, or from the meat department of a store such as Whole Foods, but if that's not an option, buy a big, free-range roasting chicken instead. As with turkey, hallowed additions such as fluffy mashed potatoes and cranberry sauce complete the picture.

6-pound capon or roasting chicken
1 onion, quartered
1 tablespoon Herbes de Provence Blend (page 101) or 1½ teaspoons dried store-bought blend
Fine sea salt and freshly ground black pepper
2 tablespoons unsalted butter, softened
Sausage and Chestnut Dressing (page 105)

3 cups gluten-free chicken broth
¼ cup medium-dry sherry
2 tablespoons cornstarch

:: **Serves 6**

1. Preheat the oven to 375°F.

2. Remove any giblets from the cavity, and rinse the capon inside and out. Pat dry with paper towels. Put the onion in a small bowl, add the Herbes de Provence Blend, and season with plenty of salt and pepper. Tip the onion and seasoning into the cavity, and tie the legs together with butcher's twine. Place the bird on a rack in a roasting pan, and smear with the butter. Cover lightly with a sheet of aluminum foil. Roast for 2 hours, and remove the foil. (If only one oven is available, add the baking dish of Sausage and Chestnut Dressing now.) Continue roasting the bird for another 20 minutes—calculating a total of 20 minutes per pound plus 20 minutes extra—until well browned and a meat thermometer inserted in the breast reads 165°F. Transfer to a warmed platter, tent loosely with foil, and let rest for 15 minutes.

3. To make the gravy: Pour the cooking juices from the roasting pan into a glass measuring cup. When the fat rises, spoon off 2 tablespoons and return to the pan. Discard the remaining fat, but reserve the clear chicken juices and blend them with the chicken broth. Place the roasting pan over medium-low heat, and add the sherry. Using a wooden spoon, scrape up the good browned bits. Add the chicken broth, and bring to a boil. Strain into a saucepan, place over medium-low heat, and simmer for 10 minutes. Blend the cornstarch with ¼ cup cold water. Stir in, and let bubble until the gravy thickens and clears, 30 seconds or less. Taste, adjust seasoning, and pour into a heated sauceboat. Carve the capon, and serve with the dressing and gravy.

sausage and chestnut dressing

SO POPULAR THAT IT upstages the holiday bird, this rich and savory dressing is baked in a casserole, since stuffing cooked inside the cavity absorbs a huge amount of rendered poultry fat. If you prefer a moist texture to a crumbly one, just add more chicken broth. Remember to make gluten-free bread for the bread crumbs ahead of time. Pine nuts can be used in lieu of chestnuts if you prefer, or if chestnuts are hard to find.

4 tablespoons (½ stick) unsalted butter

1 large onion, chopped

2 celery ribs, destringed and chopped

½ pound ground pork, crumbled

1 teaspoon minced sage or ½ teaspoon dried sage

Grated zest of ½ lemon

2 ounces pancetta, finely chopped

2½ cups soft bread crumbs made from day-old Quick White Rice Flour Flatbread (page 133)

1½ to 2 cups gluten-free chicken broth

½ cup quinoa flakes

1 cup ready-to-use roasted chestnuts, cut in half, or ¾ cup pine nuts

1. Preheat the oven to 375°F.

2. Grease an 8 × 10-inch oven-to-table baking dish with 2 tablespoons of the butter. Melt the remaining 2 tablespoons butter over medium-low heat in a large skillet. Add the onion and celery, and cook, stirring, until translucent, 7 to 8 minutes. Transfer to a plate. Increase the heat to medium, and add the pork, sage, lemon zest, and pancetta. Sauté until the pork loses its pink color, about 7 minutes, breaking it up well. Set aside.

3. Place the bread crumbs in a large bowl. Drizzle with 1½ cups of the chicken broth little by little, tossing at the same time, until evenly moistened. Add the onion and celery, sausage mixture, quinoa flakes, chestnuts, Herbes de Provence Blend, and parsley. Season to taste with salt and pepper, remembering that the chicken broth will contain

2 teaspoons Herbes de
    Provence Blend (page
    101) or 1 teaspoon
    dried store-bought
    blend
¼ cup chopped parsley
Fine sea salt and freshly
    ground black pepper

:: **Serves 6**

salt, and mix well. This makes a fairly crumbly dressing. If you prefer a moist one, add the additional ½ cup chicken broth. Spoon lightly into the baking dish, without packing. Bake, uncovered, until the top is lightly browned and crunchy, 35 to 40 minutes.

game hens with roasted tomatoes and orange rice pilaf

IT'S NOT DIFFICULT TO remove the backbone and tiresome little rib bones from a game hen, which makes it much easier to eat. Or ask your butcher to do it. Use very small tomatoes, as the skins on regular cherry tomatoes are too tough for this preparation. Trilogy rice blend (a mixture of white, brown, and wild rice) can be found in natural foods stores.

1. Preheat the oven to 350°F. Grease a roasting pan lightly with olive oil.

2. Place the tomatoes in a shallow ceramic baking dish large enough to hold them in one layer. Add half the slivered orange zest and the olive oil. Season to taste with salt and pepper. Stir to mix well, and sprinkle with the sugar.

3. Remove the backbone from each game hen by slicing through the soft rib bones on either side of it. Lay the hens on a cutting board, skin side down. Slide a sharp paring knife under the remaining rib cage of each, and cut it free. Place the now-flattened hens in the roasting pan, skin side up, and tuck the bay leaves underneath. Smear each one with 1 teaspoon butter, and season lightly with salt and pepper.

2 tablespoons extra virgin olive oil, plus extra for greasing pan

2 cups tiny tomatoes, such as Sweet 100s

Slivered zest and juice of 1 orange

Fine sea salt and freshly ground black pepper

1 teaspoon sugar

2 Rock Cornish game hens, 1¼ pounds each, preferably fresh

2 bay leaves

2 teaspoons unsalted butter, softened

1 cup gluten-free chicken broth

1 cup trilogy rice blend

¼ cup dried Zante currants

¼ cup sliced almonds, lightly toasted

:: **Serves 4**

4. Place the hens and the dish of tomatoes in the oven. Roast the hens until golden brown and the juices run clear (prick with a knife tip in the thigh meat to test), and the tomatoes are slightly wrinkled and tender, about 40 minutes.

5. Meanwhile, bring the chicken broth, orange juice, and ¾ cup water to a boil. Add the rice, currants, and remaining orange zest, reduce the heat to medium-low, cover the pan, and simmer until the rice is tender, 30 to 35 minutes. If a little liquid should remain, increase the heat and boil hard for a minute or two, stirring, until it evaporates. Just before serving, stir in the sliced almonds.

6. To serve, cut the hens in half, discarding the bay leaves. Arrange on 4 heated dinner plates with the tomatoes, which act as a sauce, and the pilaf.

ostrich burgers with red wine sauce

TODAY'S FARMED OSTRICH PRODUCES a flavorful, juicy red meat, similar in taste and texture to beef, but 90 percent fat-free, which makes it lower in cholesterol and calories than all other poultry and meats, including venison. And there's no such thing as Angry Ostrich Disease. Like other very lean meats, it's best cooked briefly. Dusting the patties with rice flour helps the browning process and gives a good surface texture. Ground ostrich meat is available frozen from upscale food markets such as Whole Foods.

8 ounces ground ostrich, at room temperature

1 egg yolk

1 large shallot, finely chopped

½ teaspoon chopped fresh thyme or ¼ teaspoon dried thyme

Fine sea salt and freshly ground black pepper

2 tablespoons extra virgin olive oil

White rice flour, for dusting

1 tablespoon brandy

½ cup red wine

Fresh thyme sprigs, optional

:: **Serves 2**

1. Crumble the ostrich meat into a bowl. Add the egg yolk, shallot, and thyme. Season with salt and pepper. Using your hands, mix lightly but thoroughly. Shape into two oval patties, each ¾ inch thick.

2. Heat the olive oil in a heavy skillet over medium heat. Dust the patties with rice flour. Brown on both sides, turning them twice to keep the juices flowing, until medium rare, about 5 minutes. Transfer to warmed plates. Add the brandy to the pan and let it sizzle for a few seconds, then add the wine. Let bubble until reduced to 4 tablespoons of liquid, stirring up any browned bits in the pan, 2 to 3 minutes, and spoon around the patties. Garnish with thyme sprigs, if using.

Meat and Seafood

TRIED-AND-TRUE COMFORT FOODS LIKE BRAISED short ribs and meat loaf don't require much tweaking to make them gluten-free, and no one ever notices the difference if a rack of lamb with a herbed crumb crust is made with rice flour bread crumbs rather than the wheat-bread kind. Fish dishes, too, are easy. In fact, simple panfried fish fillets taste better than usual when dusted with white rice flour before sautéing. As it contains no gluten, the flour doesn't become gluey, and it imparts a crisper surface texture. Quinoa goes especially well with fish and seafood, as does rice.

pork chops and baked polenta with peppers

IN THIS EASY SUPPER dish, seared bone-less pork chops finish cooking in the oven on a bed of buttery, herb-scented polenta. If you like, you can substitute fresh rosemary for oregano, or add a garnish of torn-up fresh basil leaves.

1. Preheat the oven to 400°F.

2. Pour 2 tablespoons of the butter into an 8 × 10-inch baking dish. Arrange the polenta slices in it, overlapping slightly, in three rows. Season lightly with salt and pepper, and scatter the chopped bell pepper and oregano on top. Drizzle with the remaining 2 tablespoons butter. Top with the Parmesan. Bake for about 30 minutes until bubbling and starting to brown.

3. When the polenta has baked for 15 minutes, heat the olive oil in a heavy skillet over medium-high heat until it shimmers. Pat the chops dry with paper towels, and season lightly with salt and pepper. Brown on both sides, 5 minutes. Remove the polenta from the oven, and arrange the chops on top. Add the wine to the skillet and let bubble, scraping up the browned bits on the bottom, and reduce by half,

4 tablespoons unsalted butter, melted

1 roll (16 to 18 ounces) precooked polenta, sliced ¼ inch thick

Fine sea salt and freshly ground black pepper

1 large red bell pepper, broiled, peeled, and roughly chopped, or the equivalent from a jar

1 teaspoon chopped fresh oregano or ½ teaspoon dried oregano

4 to 6 tablespoons grated Parmigiano-Reggiano

1 tablespoon extra virgin olive oil

4 boneless pork chops, 4 to 6 ounces each, 1 inch thick

¼ cup dry white wine

:: **Serves 4**

30 seconds or less. Pour the liquid over each chop. Return the baking dish to the oven and continue baking for 6 minutes until the chops are just cooked through. Cooked this way, with just a hint of pink within, they will be juicy and tender.

english pork sausage patties

THIS MIXTURE CONTAINS RICE flour bread crumbs, rather than the usual wheat rusk, to impart the characteristic smooth texture. Making your own additive-free sausage mixture using meat from a reputable butcher means that you control the freshness, the fat content, and the all-important seasonings.

1. Break the egg into a bowl, and beat lightly. Add the lemon zest (grate over the bowl if possible, to utilize the fine spray of lemon oil), nutmeg, sage, salt, pepper, and bread crumbs. Crumble the pork and veal into the mixture, and blend to a smooth paste. Moisten your hands with water and form into six ¾-inch-thick patties.

2. Heat the oil in a large, nonstick skillet over medium-low heat until it shimmers. Add the patties, and cook until brown on both sides and cooked through, about 8 minutes. Serve with mashed potatoes and mustard.

1 large egg
Grated zest of ½ lemon
½ teaspoon ground nutmeg
1 teaspoon dried sage leaves, crumbled
1 teaspoon fine sea salt
½ teaspoon freshly ground white pepper
1 cup soft white Rice Flour Bread Crumbs (page 134)
1 pound ground pork shoulder
½ pound ground veal
1 tablespoon canola oil
Mashed potatoes
Mustard

:: **Makes approximately 1½ pounds; serves 6**

meat loaf with quinoa

1 tablespoon extra virgin
    olive oil
1 onion, finely chopped
1 celery rib, destringed
    and finely chopped
¼ cup finely chopped
    fresh parsley stalks
1 teaspoon dried thyme
3 anchovy fillets, canned
    in olive oil, drained
½ cup soft white Rice
    Flour Bread Crumbs
    (page 134)
½ cup quinoa flakes
⅓ cup dry white wine or
    gluten-free beef broth
1½ pounds ground beef
    chuck
½ pound ground pork
½ pound ground veal
2 large eggs
¼ cup pistachio nuts,
    optional
1½ teaspoons fine sea
    salt
Freshly ground black
    pepper

Serves 6

THIS REWORKED CLASSIC IS good hot or cold, when it makes the best sandwiches teamed with homemade crusty rice flour bread. Lacking a 9 × 5-inch loaf pan, use an 8 × 4-inch standard pan and freeze the extra cup of meat mixture for meatballs or hamburgers.

1. Preheat the oven to 350°F. Grease a 9 × 5-inch loaf pan, preferably earthenware or heatproof glass.

2. Heat the olive oil in a skillet over medium-low heat until it shimmers. Add the onion, celery, and parsley stalks, and cook until softened but not browned, 5 minutes. Add the thyme and the anchovies, mashing them until they dissolve. (The anchovies will contribute richness, but will not impart a "fishy" taste.) Let cool to lukewarm.

3. Combine the bread crumbs and quinoa flakes in a bowl, and add the wine. Let stand until absorbed, 5 minutes. Crumble the beef, pork, and veal into the bowl, blending them into the bread crumb–quinoa mixture with your hands. Add the eggs, onion mixture, pistachios, if using, salt, and black pepper to taste, and mix well. Transfer the mixture to the loaf pan. Smooth the surface, mounding it up slightly in the center. Bake, uncovered, until the internal temperature reaches 165°F on an instant-read meat thermometer, 1 to 1¼ hours. Pour off the fat, and let rest in the pan for 10 minutes before slicing.

rack of lamb with herbed crumb crust

IT'S EASY TO ORCHESTRATE this special-occasion dish. All you have to do at the last minute is pop the prepared racks in a hot oven for 18 minutes. Unless you have an exceptional butcher, you will probably have to finish trimming the lamb yourself: using a sharp paring knife, shave off every last vestige of fat, leaving just the bones with a nubbin of tender meat at the base. Be sure to have Rice Flour Bread Crumbs (page 134) on hand for the crumb crust.

1. Heat 2 tablespoons of the olive oil in a large skillet over medium-high heat. Sear the lamb on both sides until nicely browned, about 5 minutes. Transfer to a plate, and season lightly with salt and pepper.

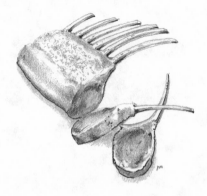

6 tablespoons extra virgin olive oil

2 racks of lamb, 7 to 8 ribs each, trimmed and frenched, all fat removed

Fine sea salt and freshly ground black pepper

1 tablespoon whole-grain Dijon mustard

2 garlic cloves, minced

2 teaspoons Herbes de Provence Blend (page 101) or 1 teaspoon dried store-bought blend

½ cup soft white Rice Flour Bread Crumbs (page 134)

3 tablespoons finely chopped parsley

:: Serves 6

2. Blend the mustard with 2 tablespoons of the olive oil, and set aside.

3. In a small skillet, heat the remaining 2 tablespoons olive oil over medium heat. Add the garlic and Herbes de Provence Blend, cook for 10 seconds, and stir in the bread crumbs. Remove from the heat, season lightly with salt and pepper, and stir in the parsley. Let cool.

4. Preheat the oven to 450°F. Place the lamb racks in a shallow roasting pan, curved side up and bone tips down. Spread the meat with the mustard mixture, and cover evenly with the crumbs. Roast until medium rare and an instant-read meat thermometer registers 135°F, about 18 minutes. Transfer the racks to a warmed platter, tent loosely with aluminum foil, and let rest for 7 to 10 minutes. Cut between the rib bones to serve, and spoon the juices over the meat.

braised short ribs with sun-dried tomatoes

THIS IS SUCCULENT, SATISFYING COMFORT FOOD for a winter evening. Most recipes suggest dredging short ribs with flour before browning, which makes an awful mess. Instead, stir brown rice flour into the softened onions. Creamy polenta or mashed potatoes are a must here.

1. Preheat the oven to 325°F. Pat the ribs dry with paper towels, and season with salt and pepper.

2. Heat the olive oil over medium heat in a large, heavy sauté pan until it shimmers. Add half the ribs, and sauté until they become a rich, dark brown, about 12 minutes. Transfer to a heavy casserole, preferably enameled cast iron. Repeat with the remaining ribs. Pour off most of the fat in the pan, leaving just a film. Add the onion, and cook until softened, 5 minutes. Sprinkle with the cinnamon and rice flour, and stir well. Add the orange juice, scraping up all the browned bits in the pan, then add the orange zest and broth. Pour over the ribs. Cover the casserole, and bake for 2 hours. Let cool and refrigerate overnight.

3. Lift off congealed fat and discard. Add the sun-dried tomatoes, and heat the ribs on top of the stove over medium-low heat. Meanwhile, bring ½ cup water to a boil in a small saucepan. Add a pinch of salt and the peas, and simmer until tender, 2 minutes. Drain.

4 pounds beef short ribs, cut into 2-inch chunks

Fine sea salt and freshly ground black pepper

2 tablespoons extra virgin olive oil

1 large onion, finely chopped

1 teaspoon ground cinnamon

3 tablespoons brown rice flour

1 cup freshly squeezed orange juice

4 strips orange zest, 2 × ½ inch

3 cups gluten-free beef broth

16 sun-dried tomatoes in oil, drained, cut in half

2 cups frozen petite peas, thawed

1 tablespoon cornstarch, optional

Hot creamy polenta or
mashed potatoes

:: **Serves 6 to 8**

4. Divide the ribs among heated plates. Taste the sauce for seasoning. There should be about 5 cups. If necessary, add a little water or boil hard to reduce it. (Alternatively, thicken by stirring in the optional cornstarch mixed with 1 tablespoon cold water, and let the sauce bubble until it thickens and clears, 20 seconds or less.) Spoon the sauce over the ribs, and garnish with the peas. Serve with polenta or mashed potatoes.

braised oxtail with mushrooms

A GREAT CHOICE FOR casual entertaining, succulent oxtail doesn't require carving or fussing over at the last minute, and doesn't spoil if the meal has to wait. Cook it a day ahead, so you can remove the fat easily, and serve with mashed potatoes for absorbing the rich sauce.

1. Preheat the oven to 400°F. Grease a roasting pan with 1 tablespoon of the olive oil, and arrange the oxtail pieces in it in a single layer, slightly separated. Roast, turning once, until well browned, about 30 minutes.

2. Heat the remaining 2 tablespoons olive oil in a large, heavy pot over medium heat. Add the onion, and sauté until softened but not colored, 5 minutes. Add the carrot, garlic, orange zest, thyme, tomato paste, and wine. Bring to a simmer. Using tongs, add the oxtail to the pot. Place the roasting pan over medium heat, and deglaze with the beef stock, scraping up the browned bits with a wooden spoon. Add to the pot, and season to taste with salt and pepper. Cover and simmer gently until the meat is very tender and comes away from the bones easily, adding more stock as needed, 3½ to 4 hours. Let cool, then refrigerate overnight.

3. Remove the meat from the refrigerator, lift off the layer of congealed fat, and discard it. Reheat the oxtail gently, bringing it to a low boil. (Try a piece of meat to make

3 tablespoons extra virgin olive oil
4 pounds oxtail, sliced 2 inches thick
1 onion, chopped
1 carrot, diced
2 garlic cloves, chopped
Zest of ½ orange, slivered
3 sprigs fresh thyme
1 tablespoon tomato paste
1½ cups red wine
1½ to 2 cups gluten-free beef stock
Fine sea salt and freshly ground black pepper
1 tablespoon unsalted butter
¾ pound white mushrooms, thickly sliced
2 cloves garlic, minced
1 tablespoon cornstarch
3 tablespoons chopped parsley

:: **Serves 4 to 6**

sure it is warmed through.) Blend the cornstarch with 2 tablespoons water, stir into the meat, and continue cooking until the sauce thickens and clears, 20 seconds or less.

4. Melt the butter over medium heat until it foams. Add the mushrooms and garlic, and sauté until glassy-looking and cooked through, 5 minutes. Season lightly with salt and pepper.

5. Divide the oxtail and sauce among heated dinner plates, top with the mushrooms, and sprinkle with parsley. Serve with mashed potatoes.

nut-crusted salmon with mustard cream sauce

CHOPPED NUTS RATHER THAN crisp bread crumbs offer flavor as well as texture to baked salmon fillets. Small specialty potatoes such as fingerlings or Dutch Gold, boiled in their jackets, make a good accompaniment and are enhanced by the voluptuous sauce.

1. Preheat the oven to 400°F.

2. Line a shallow baking pan with aluminum foil, and lay the salmon fillets on it, skin side down, at least 1 inch apart. Blend the olive oil and mustard together, and spread one-quarter on top of each portion. Top with the chopped pecans. Bake until just cooked through, about 10 minutes.

3. While the salmon bakes, make the sauce: Whip the cream until it starts to stiffen, then whip in the mustard. Stir in the capers and parsley. Season to taste with salt and pepper.

4. Transfer the salmon to heated dinner plates. Garnish each fillet with a big dollop of the sauce.

4 salmon fillets, about 6 ounces each
3 tablespoons extra virgin olive oil
3 tablespoons Dijon mustard
6 tablespoons chopped pecans

MUSTARD AND CAPER SAUCE
½ cup heavy cream
1 tablespoon Dijon mustard
1 tablespoon drained capers, rinsed
2 tablespoons finely chopped parsley
Fine sea salt and freshly ground black pepper

:: **Serves 4**

halibut, tomato, and caper gratin with quinoa

2 tablespoons extra
virgin olive oil, plus
extra for baking dish
½ cup soft white Rice
Flour Bread Crumbs
(page 134)
4 halibut steaks, about
6 ounces each
Fine sea salt and freshly
ground black pepper
½ teaspoon fennel
seeds, crushed
1 large can (28 ounces)
diced tomatoes,
drained, juice reserved
2 tablespoons drained
capers, rinsed
1½ cups yellow quinoa

∷ **Serves 4**

THIS QUICKLY MADE SUPPER dish uses any firm white fish fillets such as cod, orange roughy, or snapper.

1. Preheat the oven to 350°F. Grease an 8 × 10-inch baking dish with olive oil.
2. Heat the olive oil in a small skillet over medium-low heat, add the bread crumbs, and stir until well coated, 30 seconds. Set aside.
3. Arrange the fish in the baking dish, and season with salt, pepper, and the fennel seeds. Top with the diced tomatoes, capers, and reserved bread crumbs. Drizzle with a little more olive oil. Bake until the fish is opaque and flakes easily, 20 minutes.
4. Meanwhile, rinse the quinoa. Combine the reserved tomato juice with enough water to make 3 cups. Bring to a boil, and stir in the quinoa with ½ teaspoon salt. Cover, reduce the heat to low, and simmer until tender and the liquid evaporates, 15 minutes. Serve with the fish.

halibut in foil with brown basmati rice

HERE'S A FOOLPROOF WAY to cook fish, and there's no pan to wash afterward. Aromatic brown basmati rice complements the flavors and textures of the halibut perfectly. The fish takes only 10 minutes to cook, so start the rice first. The recipe can be doubled with ease, but don't try baking more than four halibut packages at once in the average home oven. The temperature will drop too much under the onslaught and throw the timing off.

1. Rinse the rice, and drain. Bring 1½ cups water to a boil in a small saucepan, and add the salt and rice. Cover, reduce the heat to low, and simmer until the rice is tender, about 30 minutes. Fluff with a fork, cover, and let stand for 10 minutes. Heat the butter in a small skillet over medium-low heat, add the sliced almonds, and cook until golden, 1 to 2 minutes. Stir into the rice when ready to serve.

2. Preheat the oven to 400°F. Heat a baking sheet at the same time.

3. While the rice cooks, prepare the fish packages: Heat the olive oil in a small skillet over medium heat and sauté the onion until softened, 5 minutes. Remove from the heat, and add the orange zest and sherry.

¾ cup brown basmati rice

½ teaspoon fine sea salt

2 tablespoons unsalted butter

5 tablespoons sliced almonds

1 tablespoon extra virgin olive oil

1 small onion, thinly sliced

2 teaspoons slivered orange zest

2 tablespoons medium-dry sherry

2 halibut steaks, about 6 ounces each

Salt and freshly ground white pepper

Large pinch of nutmeg, freshly grated

Chopped parsley

:: **Serves 2**

4. Lay two 12 × 16-inch sheets of aluminum foil on a work surface and spoon one-quarter of the onion mixture on each sheet, arranging it off-center. Place the halibut on top, and season with salt and pepper to taste. Sprinkle with the nutmeg, and spread with the remaining onion mixture. Fold the foil over the fish like closing a book, then crimp the open edges tightly together to form two flat, rectangular packages.

5. Place the halibut packages on the hot baking sheet, and bake for 10 minutes. Transfer to dinner plates, and slit open along the uncrimped side. (If the fillets are extra thick and the fish does not flake easily, return opened packages to the oven for a few more minutes.) Pull away the foil, leaving the halibut and sauce on the plates. Spoon the rice alongside, and scatter parsley on top.

garlic shrimp with saffron rice

EVEN FROZEN SHRIMP ARE delicious when cooked this way. Start cooking the rice while the shrimp marinate.

1. Arrange the shrimp in a shallow baking dish large enough to hold them in one layer (or use two dishes). Top with 4 tablespoons of the olive oil, the lemon juice, garlic, parsley, tarragon, ½ teaspoon of the salt, and a generous grinding of pepper. Turn them all over to coat well, and let stand at room temperature for 20 minutes.

2. Meanwhile, heat the remaining 2 tablespoons olive oil in a small saucepan over medium-low heat until it shimmers. Add the onion and cook, stirring frequently, until it softens and turns translucent, about 5 minutes. Add the rice, stirring well to coat the grains. Add the saffron mixture, 2¾ cups hot water, and the remaining ¾ teaspoon salt, and bring to a boil. Cover the pan, reduce the heat to low, and simmer until tender, 17 minutes. Remove from the heat, fluff with a fork, and partially cover the pan until the shrimp are ready.

3. Preheat the oven to 400°F. Bake the shrimp until opaque and cooked through, 10 minutes. Serve with the rice, spooning the flavorful juices on top.

1½ pounds shelled and deveined large shrimp, thawed if frozen

6 tablespoons extra virgin olive oil

1 tablespoon lemon juice

2 garlic cloves, minced

2 tablespoons finely chopped parsley

1 teaspoon dried tarragon, crumbled

1¼ teaspoon fine sea salt

Freshly ground black pepper

1 medium onion, finely chopped

1½ cups long-grain white rice

½ teaspoon saffron threads, steeped in 1 tablespoon hot water

∷ **Serves 4**

five-minute trout with crispy caper sauce

2 whole boned trout,
  6 to 8 ounces each
4 tablespoons extra
  virgin olive oil
Fine sea salt and freshly
  ground black pepper
2 tablespoons soft
  white Rice Flour Bread
  Crumbs (page 134)
2 tablespoons capers,
  rinsed and drained
2 tablespoons lemon
  juice
2 tablespoons chopped
  parsley

:: **Serves 2**

WHEN BONED TROUT ARE spread out flat and broiled, skin side up to protect the tender flesh, they cook to a turn in just 5 minutes. As one whole butterflied trout covers an entire dinner plate, serve with homemade crusty rice flour bread and have a salad or green vegetable as a separate course.

1. Remove the rack of the broiler pan and cover it with aluminum foil.

2. Preheat the broiler.

3. Rinse the trout and pat dry. Place on the foil-wrapped broiler rack, spread out flat with the flesh side up. Brush with 1 tablespoon of the olive oil, season with salt and pepper, and then turn the trout skin side up. Broil until cooked through (the skin will blacken and blister, but will keep the fish moist), about 5 minutes. Transfer to heated dinner plates, placing them skin side down.

4. Meanwhile, heat the remaining 3 tablespoons olive oil in a small skillet over medium-low heat. Add the bread crumbs, and sauté until golden brown and crispy, 20 seconds. Remove from the heat, stir in the capers and lemon juice, and season lightly with salt and pepper. Spoon half the mixture over each trout. Scatter the chopped parsley on top.

Breads

DEVELOPING EASY RECIPES FOR ARTISAN-STYLE loaves using gluten-free flours was a challenge, but a rewarding one. Technically, the recipes that follow are all batter breads: the dough is mixed rather than kneaded, and all but one are raised with baking powder, not yeast. This means you can produce an aromatic, crusty loaf with a light, elastic crumb in about 30 minutes, even if you've never baked a loaf of bread in your life.

Based on the hearth breads of old, most of these loaves are quite small and relatively low, because gluten-free flours don't form the weblike, airy structure that characterizes bread made with milled wheat and yeast. But what they lack in size they make up for in flavor, texture, and nutrition. Xanthan gum, a white powder derived from corn syrup, helps to promote a springy texture and retain moisture. True, these preservative-free breads don't keep (neither do baguettes from a French bakery), but they freeze well.

quick brown rice flour flatbread

THIS MELLOW-TASTING, VERSATILE whole-grain bread is perfect with cheese or with butter and jam for breakfast. Small, round, and crusty, like old-fashioned hearth breads, these loaves can be sliced across or split and quartered for sandwiches.

1. Preheat the oven to 400°F. Line a large baking sheet with parchment paper. Combine the rice flour and almonds in a food processor, and grind to a fine meal. Add the tapioca starch, flaxmeal, anise seeds, salt, baking powder, baking soda, and xanthan gum, and process to mix.

2. Combine the yogurt, canola oil, egg, and ½ cup water in a bowl. Add the liquid ingredients to the dry ingredients all at once, and process to form a fluffy-looking, sticky batter, about 30 seconds. Scooping out the batter with a rubber spatula, form two equal mounds on the baking sheet, 5 inches apart. Sprinkle lightly with rice flour, and pat each one gently into a 6-inch disk. Form a rounded edge by dipping your fingers in rice flour and nudging the sides of the dough. Using a long knife blade, cut a diagonal grid pattern on top of each flatbread, making three ¼-inch-deep cuts each way. Bake until golden brown and crusty, about 25 minutes. Transfer the loaves to a wire rack and let cool.

¾ cup brown rice flour, plus additional for forming loaves
½ cup almonds
¾ cup tapioca starch
2 tablespoons flaxmeal
¼ teaspoon anise seeds
½ teaspoon fine sea salt
1 teaspoon baking powder
1 teaspoon baking soda
1 teaspoon xanthan gum
½ cup plain whole milk yogurt
1 tablespoon canola oil
1 large egg

:: **Makes 2 flatbreads**

Parchment Paper Versus Wax Paper

Lining a baking sheet with parchment paper helps to prevent overbrowning on the underside of breads and cookies; baked items don't stick to it, it's reusable within reason, and it saves a lot of washing up. Parchment is available in natural foods stores, kitchenware shops, and some supermarkets. Wax paper is not a substitute. Basically tissue paper that's been coated with paraffin wax on both sides, wax paper was originally invented for wrapping foods (think of sandwich packets in the days before plastic bags) and was never meant for baking. The wax melts.

quick white rice flour flatbread

LIKE ITS WHOLE-GRAIN TWIN on page 131, this low, round loaf has a hundred uses, including pizza, melba toast, croutons, and—most important—bread crumbs. These are more valuable than gold in the wheat-free kitchen for breading, topping gratins, and making stuffings. This loaf is very good sliced and toasted under a broiler (don't share the family toaster if it's ever used for wheat products). The biscotti-shaped slices are marvelous for dipping in soft-boiled eggs.

1. Preheat the oven to 400°F. Line a large baking sheet with parchment paper. Combine the rice flour and almonds in a food processor, and grind to a fine meal. Add the tapioca starch, salt, baking powder, baking soda, and xanthan gum, and process to mix.

³/₄ cup white rice flour, plus additional for forming loaves

¹/₂ cup blanched, slivered almonds

³/₄ cup tapioca starch

³/₄ teaspoon fine sea salt

1 teaspoon baking powder

1 teaspoon baking soda

1 teaspoon xanthan gum

1 tablespoon canola oil

¹/₂ cup plain whole milk yogurt

1 large egg

.: **Makes 2 flatbreads**

2. Combine the canola oil, yogurt, egg, and ½ cup water. Add the liquid ingredients to the dry ingredients all at once, and process to form a fluffy-looking, sticky batter, about 20 seconds. Scooping out the batter with a rubber spatula, form two equal mounds on the baking sheet, 5 inches apart. Sprinkle lightly with rice flour, and pat each one gently into a 6-inch disk. Form a rounded edge by dipping your fingers in rice flour and nudging the sides of the dough. Slash the top of each flatbread from side to side, forming a cross. Bake until golden brown and crusty, about 25 minutes. Transfer the loaves to a wire rack and let cool.

RICE FLOUR BREAD CRUMBS

Bake the bread as above, and leave at room temperature overnight. Cut off the crusts and reserve. Dice the soft interior, transfer to a food processor, and process to form soft, coarse crumbs. Process the crusts separately to make fine dry crumbs, which are ideal for breading. Store both types, in plastic bags, in the freezer.

rice flour english muffins

I SUSPECT THAT REGULAR English muffins owe much of their popularity to the amount of butter melting on their toasted surfaces; on their own, they're far from interesting. These gluten-free English muffins, on the other hand, are worth nibbling even when unadorned. Suitably thick but light and airy (the batter is rich with eggs), they have the requisite floury outer surface and holey interior, take only 10 minutes to bake, and toast beautifully. To make them, you'll need muffin rings, or simply use recycled cat-food cans (the 6½-ounce size) with the tops and bottoms removed. The recipe is easy to double.

Unsalted butter
⅔ cup white rice flour, plus extra for muffin rings and griddle
⅓ cup tapioca starch
1 teaspoon sugar
1 teaspoon baking soda
Pinch of fine sea salt
2 large eggs
1 tablespoon canola oil
½ cup plain whole milk yogurt

:: **Makes 5 muffins**

1. Butter the insides of five 3½-inch muffin rings, and dust with rice flour. (Dipping them in the flour is the easiest way to do this.)
2. Combine the rice flour, tapioca starch, sugar, baking soda, and salt. In a separate bowl, beat the eggs, and whisk in the canola oil and yogurt.
3. Place a nonstick griddle (or two nonstick skillets) over medium-low heat, and set the muffin rings in place. Sprinkle a little rice flour on the griddle surface inside each one to prevent the muffins from sticking.

4. When the griddle is hot, add the liquid ingredients to the flour mixture, and stir well to form a puffy batter. Half-fill each muffin ring, smoothing the surface, and dust lightly with additional rice flour. After 1 minute, nudge each muffin ring with a spatula to make sure it isn't sticking, and continue cooking for another 3 minutes. Holding tongs in one hand and a spatula in the other, pick up each ring (the muffin won't fall out) and place on the spatula. Reverse the muffins back onto the griddle and continue cooking until the second side is browned and the muffin is cooked through, 3 to 4 minutes. Transfer to a rack. When the rings are cool enough to handle, free the muffins with a knife blade, and let cool completely. Split (never cut!) by inserting the tines of a fork horizontally around each muffin, and pry apart for optimal cragginess; then toast under a broiler. The muffins will keep for 2 days wrapped and refrigerated, or they may be frozen.

goat cheese pizza with rice flour crust

THE WHITE RICE FLOUR flatbread on page 133 makes a good base for pizza. This goat cheese topping always wins approval, but of course you can use any pizza topping you like.

1. Preheat the oven to 400°F. Line a large baking sheet with parchment paper.

2. Using a rubber spatula, divide the flatbread dough into two equal mounds on the baking sheet, 5 inches apart. Flatten each one gently into an 8-inch disk, making the rim slightly thicker. Bake until firm but not browned, 15 minutes.

3. Remove the pizza bases from the oven, and spread each one with marinara sauce to within 1 inch of the rim. Top with dollops of goat cheese, the tomatoes, oregano, anchovies, olives, and onion rings. Return to the oven, and bake until the pizza edges are crisp and golden, a further 15 minutes.

RICE FLOUR FOCACCIA

To make focaccia, proceed as above, making two equal mounds of dough on the baking sheet. Flatten into 8-inch disks. Spray or brush with olive oil, and sprinkle with coarse sea salt or kosher salt crystals and chopped fresh herbs, such as rosemary, oregano, or thyme. Bake until golden, about 20 minutes.

1 recipe Quick White Rice Flour Flatbread (page 133), unbaked

8 tablespoons marinara sauce (from a jar or can)

4 ounces soft white goat cheese

2 or 3 Roma tomatoes, sliced

½ teaspoon dried oregano

4 anchovy fillets canned in olive oil, drained and coarsely chopped

½ cup black oil-cured olives, halved and pitted

½ red onion, thinly sliced and separated into rings

:: **Makes two 8-inch pizzas**

rice flour baguettes

½ cup white rice flour
½ cup blanched
   almonds, whole
   or slivered, lightly
   toasted
½ cup tapioca starch
¾ teaspoon fine sea salt
1½ teaspoons baking
   powder
½ cup plain whole milk
   yogurt
2 large egg whites
Coarse salt crystals

Makes 2 baguettes

THESE LONG, THIN, CRISP-CRUSTED baguettes have a light and chewy interior thanks to beaten egg whites in the dough. Unusually, no xanthan gum is needed. The unbaked dough is soft and needs support; to form these long loaves you will need a double baguette pan, which looks like an 18-inch-long drainpipe sliced in half vertically and stuck together to make a *W*. They can be found in most kitchenware shops.

For super sandwiches, split the baguettes, spread with grainy Dijon mustard, and fill with Ground Chicken Roll with Quinoa (page 89) and mixed baby greens.

1. Preheat the oven to 400°F. Line a double baguette pan with a sheet of parchment paper, creasing the outer edges to make it lie snugly against the curved sides.
2. Combine the rice flour and almonds in a food processor, and grind to a fine meal. Transfer to a large bowl, and add the tapioca starch, salt, and baking powder. Combine the yogurt with ¼ cup water. In a separate bowl, beat the egg whites until stiff peaks form.
3. Add the yogurt and water to the dry ingredients, and mix well. Using a rubber spatula, stir in one-third of the egg whites, then fold in the remainder. Drop adjoining dollops of dough into the baguette pan, trying not to

hit the sides of the pan, forming two 12- to 14-inch-long loaves. Sprinkle lightly with coarse salt crystals. Bake until golden brown, about 25 minutes, then turn the loaves over, and bake another 5 minutes. Transfer the loaves to a wire rack. Serve warm. (Baguettes may be frozen and reheated.)

rustic seed bread

½ cup buckwheat flour
¼ cup flaxmeal
¾ cup brown rice flour
¼ cup tapioca starch
1 teaspoon xanthan gum
1 teaspoon baking
  powder
1 teaspoon baking soda
1 teaspoon fine sea salt
2 teaspoons caraway
  seeds
2 large eggs
½ cup plain whole milk
  yogurt
1 tablespoon molasses
1 egg white, lightly
  beaten
2 teaspoons sesame
  seeds

:: **Makes 1 flatbread**

REMINISCENT OF AN ARTISANAL rye bread, but more mellow, this close-grained dark bread is marvelous with cream cheese and Medjool dates . . . or cream cheese and smoked salmon . . . or unsalted butter and preserves.

1. Preheat the oven to 400°F. Line a baking sheet with parchment paper.

2. Combine the buckwheat flour, flaxmeal, rice flour, tapioca starch, xanthan gum, baking powder, baking soda, salt, and caraway seeds, and stir well. In a separate bowl, beat together the eggs, yogurt, molasses, and ¼ cup water. Pour the liquid ingredients over the flour mixture, and beat with a wooden spoon until smooth, 20 seconds. The dough should just hold its shape, but if it seems too firm, add 1 or 2 tablespoons more water.

Using a rubber spatula, scoop out the batter into a ball on the baking sheet. With lightly oiled hands, pat very gently (so you don't press out the air) into a 7-inch-diameter shallow dome. Brush with the egg white and sprinkle the sesame seeds evenly on top. Press them in gently.

3. Using a long knife blade and wiping it between cuts, slash a diagonal grid pattern on top of the flatbread, making four or five ¼-inch-deep cuts each way. Bake until brown and crusty, 30 minutes. Let cool on a wire rack.

Flaxseeds::

Flax is the common name for a plant with pretty blue flowers that has been cultivated for millennia, both for its long, silky fibers—used to spin linen thread—and for its seeds, which are pressed for their high oil content. (In the past, this oil was all turned into inedible linseed oil for industrial uses.) The solid residue, linseed cake, was and still is used as a nourishing feed for cattle. It's only recently that researchers have discovered that flaxseeds make an invaluable food for people, too.

Aside from their high fiber content (a paltry quarter cup contains 6 grams), flaxseeds contain huge amounts of two compounds that may confer all kinds of other medical benefits: lignans, which have improved the lot of laboratory mice with tumors, and alpha-linolenic acid, a plant-based version of the omega-3 fats that are said to help ward off heart attacks.

These beneficial seeds, which have a pleasant, grassy flavor, can be golden or brown. They keep well at room temperature, but flaxmeal should be stored in the refrigerator or freezer or it will go rancid. Flaxmeal is available at natural foods stores and some supermarkets; you can also grind your own in an electric coffee mill kept for grinding things other than coffee. Don't use a food processor: the seeds simply whirl about, because the outer seed casing is extremely hard. A wonderful addition to gluten-free breads, which can quickly turn dry, flaxmeal's high oil content keeps them moist as well as flavorful.

flaxmeal skillet bread

MADE LIKE OLD-FASHIONED CORN bread in a preheated iron skillet, this whole-grain bread has a light, supple crumb. It bakes in just 12 minutes, and goes especially well with salads and cheese.

1. Preheat the oven to 450°F, and heat a heavy, well-seasoned 8½-inch iron skillet or crêpe pan at the same time.

2. Combine the flaxmeal, rice flour, tapioca starch, baking powder, baking soda, xanthan gum, and salt. In a separate bowl, whisk together the buttermilk, egg, and 1 tablespoon of the canola oil.

3. Protecting your hand with a mitt, remove the hot skillet from the oven. Add the remaining tablespoon oil and swirl it around to coat the bottom of the pan.

4. Pour the liquid ingredients into the dry ingredients, mix until smooth, and scrape the batter into the hot, oiled skillet. Transfer to the oven and bake until brown and crusty, 12 minutes. Flip the bread out onto a wire rack, and let cool for 10 minutes before cutting into wedges.

¼ cup flaxmeal
½ cup brown rice flour
¼ cup tapioca starch
½ teaspoon baking powder
½ teaspoon baking soda
½ teaspoon xanthan gum
¼ teaspoon fine sea salt
¾ cup buttermilk or
  ½ cup plain whole
  milk yogurt plus
  ¼ cup milk
1 large egg
2 tablespoons canola oil

:: **Makes 1 flatbread**

quick flaxseed and
chickpea baguette

½ cup flaxmeal

½ cup chickpea
  (garbanzo) flour

½ cup brown rice flour

½ cup tapioca starch

1 teaspoon xanthan gum

1 tablespoon baking
  powder

½ teaspoon fine sea salt

¼ teaspoon anise seeds

1 tablespoon extra virgin
  olive oil

1 teaspoon molasses

1 large egg

½ teaspoon sesame
  seeds

Makes 1 baguette

REMINISCENT OF AN ARTISAN-MADE rustic loaf, this torpedo-shaped whole-grain loaf has a crisp crust, a soft crumb, and layers of enticing flavors. It toasts well, and makes excellent French toast.

1. Preheat the oven to 400°F. Line a large baking sheet with parchment paper.

2. In a food processor or a large bowl, combine the flaxmeal, chickpea flour, rice flour, tapioca starch, xanthan gum, baking powder, salt, and anise seeds. Process until well mixed, 10 seconds, or stir well. In a separate bowl, combine the olive oil, molasses, egg, and 1 cup water, and stir to blend.

3. Add the liquid ingredients to the dry ingredients all at once, and process long enough to form a firm, sticky batter, about 20 seconds, or beat hard with a wooden spoon for 2 minutes. Using a rubber spatula, scoop out the batter in large dollops and drop them, touching each other, in a diagonal line across the baking sheet. Using the spatula, form gently into a 14-inch-long torpedo shape with humps. Do this as lightly as possible so as not to press air out of the batter. Sprinkle with the sesame seeds. Bake until brown and crusty, about 25 minutes. Transfer the loaf to a wire rack and let cool. (See illustration on page 129.)

yeast-raised cornmeal flatbread

THESE AROMATIC, GOLDEN LOAVES are crusty on the outside and tender within. For a change of pace, you can replace the cornmeal with buckwheat, chickpea, teff, or millet flour.

1. Line a large baking sheet with parchment paper.

2. Combine ½ cup of the rice flour and the yeast with ½ cup warm (110°F) water. Let rest until doubled in volume, about 10 minutes.

3. In a large bowl, combine the remaining ½ cup rice flour, the cornmeal, tapioca starch, xanthan gum, and salt. In a separate bowl, beat the eggs lightly with 1 cup warm water and the olive oil. Stir into the flour mixture. Add the yeast mixture, and beat until smooth, about 1 minute.

4. Using a rubber spatula, make two equal mounds on the baking sheet, 5 inches apart. Flatten each one gently into an 8-inch disk, heaping it up slightly in the center. Cover the loaves lightly with greased plastic wrap, and let rise until doubled in bulk, about 1 hour.

5. Preheat the oven to 425°F. Blend the egg yolk with 1 teaspoon water, and brush over the loaves. Dust very lightly with rice flour. Using a long knife blade and wiping it between cuts, slash a diagonal grid pattern on top of each flatbread, making four or five ¼-inch-deep cuts each way. Bake until golden brown, about 25 minutes. Transfer to a wire rack. Serve warm.

1 cup brown rice flour, plus extra for dusting loaves

1½ teaspoons granular yeast

1 cup cornmeal

½ cup tapioca starch

1¼ teaspoons xanthan gum

1 teaspoon fine sea salt

2 large eggs, at room temperature

2 tablespoons extra virgin olive oil

1 egg yolk, for glaze

:: **Makes 2 flatbreads**

cornmeal and cheese shortbread

1/3 cup unsalted butter, softened

1 large egg

3/4 cup grated Cheddar, Asiago, or Romano

1 cup masa harina (Mexican corn flour for making tortillas), plus extra for rolling

1 teaspoon baking powder

Pinch of fine sea salt

3 tablespoons milk

Makes 1; serves 4 to 6

JUST RIGHT FOR NIBBLING with a glass of wine, this dappled gold disk falls somewhere between a soft, outsized Mexican tortilla and tender cheese pastry. Tear off chunks or, if this seems too casual, cut it into wedges. Serve plain or with salsa.

1. Preheat the oven to 375°F. Have ready a sheet of aluminum foil and a cookie sheet.

2. Cream the butter, and beat in the egg and cheese. Blend together the masa, baking powder, and salt. Stir into the cheese mixture little by little, alternating with sprinkles of milk, to form a soft dough. Dust the foil lightly with masa, and turn out the dough onto it. Gather it into a ball, and knead for a minute or two until smooth. Dust with a little more masa, and roll into a 10-inch circle, about 1/4 inch thick. Slide a cookie sheet under the foil, and place in the oven. Bake for 10 minutes until the pancake starts to brown at the edges.

3. Meanwhile, preheat the broiler. Place the cookie sheet under the heat, and broil until the top surface is dappled brown and gold, about 5 minutes. Serve hot.

cornmeal and sun-dried tomato loaf

THIS APPETIZING, SAVORY LOAF makes good use of the flavorful olive oil from a jar of sun-dried tomatoes. If the tomatoes remaining in the jar are left high and dry, cover them with fresh olive oil.

1. Preheat the oven to 375°F. Grease an 8½ × 4½-inch loaf pan with a little olive oil from the jar of sun-dried tomatoes.

2. Combine the cornmeal, rice flour, cornstarch, salt, oregano, baking powder, baking soda, and xanthan gum, and mix well. In a separate bowl, beat the eggs lightly, and add the tomato-flavored olive oil, milk, yogurt, and ½ cup of the Parmesan. Add the liquid ingredients to the flour mixture, and beat with a wooden spoon until smooth, 1 minute. Stir in the chopped sun-dried tomatoes. Transfer the batter to the loaf pan, smooth the top, and sprinkle with the remaining tablespoon Parmesan. Bake until risen and browned, and an inserted toothpick emerges clean, about 45 minutes. Turn out onto a wire rack and let cool before slicing.

8 sun-dried Roma tomatoes in olive oil, drained and chopped

½ cup cornmeal

½ cup brown rice flour

½ cup cornstarch

1 teaspoon fine sea salt

½ teaspoon dried oregano

1½ teaspoons baking powder

1 teaspoon baking soda

1 teaspoon xanthan gum

2 large eggs

2 tablespoons flavored olive oil from jar of sun-dried tomatoes

½ cup milk

½ cup plain whole milk yogurt

½ cup plus 1 tablespoon freshly grated Parmigiano-Reggiano

:: **Makes 1 loaf**

Cookies and Bars

IN AMERICA'S MELTING POT OF culinary traditions, there are really two kinds of cookies: the satisfying cookie-with-a-glass-of-milk variety, and the smaller, more elegant kind that goes so well with a cup of tea or espresso, or provides a crunchy counterpoint to creamy desserts. Both types have their merits, both turn out exceptionally well when made with rice, teff, and nut flours, and both are eminently gift-worthy.

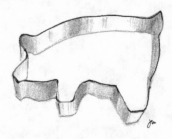

peanut butter–chocolate chip cookies

SOFT, DELECTABLE, AND OUTRAGEOUSLY rich, these confections cause cookie lovers to swoon. Use premium chocolate chips if possible. Ghirardelli make some with 60 percent cocoa butter, and they are worth seeking out for their silky smoothness.

1. Preheat the oven to 350°F. Line two large baking sheets with parchment paper. (If using only one baking sheet, cool under running water and dry before reusing, as it must be cold.)

2. Using a wooden spoon, cream the butter until smooth. Beat in the peanut butter, then the egg. Add the brown sugar, rice flour, salt, and baking powder, and stir to blend.

3. Stir in the chocolate chips and chopped nuts. The dough will be soft and sticky. Drop by the rounded tablespoon onto the baking sheets, 2 inches apart, using a second tablespoon to shape the dough into a ball and dislodge it. Bake until golden and just set, 12 to 15 minutes. Let stand on the baking sheets for 5 minutes before transferring to a wire rack to cool completely.

4 tablespoons (½ stick) unsalted butter, softened

¾ cup creamy peanut butter

1 large egg

½ cup packed dark brown sugar

¼ cup brown rice flour

Pinch of fine sea salt

¼ teaspoon baking powder

½ cup 60% dark chocolate chips

½ cup chopped pecans or walnuts

:: **Makes about 20**

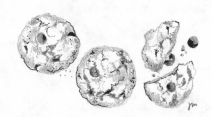

chocolate-pine nut meringue cookies

2 large egg whites
½ cup sugar
Pinch of fine sea salt
½ teaspoon vanilla
  extract
⅔ cup (3 ounces) pine
  nuts
4 ounces 60% to
  70% dark chocolate,
  melted and cooled to
  lukewarm

:: **Makes about 30**

IN ITALY, COOKIES LIKE these are known as *brutti ma buoni* (ugly but good). Quick and easy to make, they have crackly tops and chewy, rich interiors.

1. Preheat the oven to 350°F. Line a large baking sheet with parchment paper.

2. Beat the egg whites until they start to hold their shape, then beat in the sugar a little at a time. Continue beating until the meringue holds stiff, unwavering peaks, about 2 minutes. Beat in the salt and vanilla. Fold in the pine nuts, and then the chocolate. (It's fine to leave swirls.) Drop by teaspoonfuls onto the baking sheet, 1 inch apart. Bake until puffed up and crisp, about 10 minutes. (The interiors will firm up slightly as they cool.) Transfer to a wire rack.

pecan-espresso cookies

THESE BUTTERY, COFFEE-FLAVORED SHORTBREAD cookies are rolled in chopped pecans before baking for additional crunch.

1. Preheat the oven to 300°F. Line two large baking sheets with parchment paper. (If using only one baking sheet, cool under running water and dry before reusing, as it must be cold.)

2. Combine the brown sugar and butter in a food processor. Process to a smooth, fluffy cream, add the egg yolk, and process to mix. Add the rice flour, cornstarch, salt, and instant coffee, and process briefly to form a ball of soft dough.

3. Spread the chopped pecans on a work surface. Dipping your fingers in rice flour, form the dough into 1-inch balls, and roll in the chopped nuts. Flatten lightly so that the nuts stick. Transfer to the baking sheets 1½ inches apart, and chill for 10 minutes. Bake until light tan and just set, 18 minutes. Transfer to a wire rack and let cool.

½ cup packed dark brown sugar

12 tablespoons (1½ sticks) unsalted butter, cut up

1 large egg yolk

1 cup brown rice flour, plus additional for rolling cookies

¾ cup cornstarch

Pinch of fine sea salt

2 teaspoons instant coffee, preferably espresso

1 cup (4 ounces) pecans, finely chopped

:: **Makes about 30**

hazelnut zebra cookies

1 cup (4 ounces)
   hazelnuts
⅓ cup sugar
½ cup brown rice flour
½ cup cornstarch
Pinch of fine sea salt
8 tablespoons (1 stick)
   unsalted butter, cold,
   cut up
1 large egg yolk
½ teaspoon vanilla
   extract
2 ounces 60% dark
   chocolate, melted

:: **Makes about 30**

THESE LIGHT, AUSTRIAN-STYLE COOKIES rise even though they contain no baking powder because tiny granules of cold butter melt as the cookies bake and make little air spaces.

1. Preheat the oven to 325°F. Line a large baking sheet with parchment paper.

2. In the bowl of a food processor, combine the hazelnuts and sugar. Process until finely ground. Add the rice flour, cornstarch, salt, and butter. Process until the mixture starts to clump together, about 30 seconds, then add the egg yolk and vanilla, and process until the dough forms a rough ball, scraping down the bowl if necessary.

3. Pinch off small pieces of dough, and form into 1-inch balls. Flatten slightly and arrange on the baking sheet, 1 inch apart. Refrigerate for 10 minutes.

4. Bake until very lightly colored and the undersides turn a pale tan, about 15 minutes. Let firm up on the baking sheet for 2 minutes, then transfer to a wire rack and let cool.

5. Line a work surface with a sheet of aluminum foil, and place the rack of cookies on top. Push the cookies close together so they touch. Drizzle the melted chocolate off a spoon over the cookies, passing it back and forth to make random, thin stripes. Push the cookies apart, and let stand until the chocolate hardens, about 1 hour, or refrigerate for 10 minutes.

hazelnut-raspberry cookies

THE EASIEST AND QUICKEST way to get the jam filling into these miniature jam tartlets is to use a disposable cone-shaped pastry bag or, failing that, a plastic bag with a small piece snipped off one corner.

1. Preheat the oven to 375°F. Line a large baking sheet with baking parchment.

2. Separate the egg, reserving the yolk. Place the white in a shallow bowl, and beat lightly.

3. Cream the butter and brown sugar until fluffy, then beat in the vanilla and egg yolk. Add the rice flour, cornstarch, and salt, and blend thoroughly.

4. Pinch off pieces of dough and roll into 1-inch balls. Dip each ball into the egg white, and then roll in the chopped hazelnuts. Place on the prepared baking sheet. With the end of a wooden spoon, make an indentation in the center of each ball. Fill each three-quarters full with jam; set the bag with the jam aside. Bake the cookies until lightly browned, 12 to 15 minutes. Refill each cookie with jam (the filling will have "shrunk" slightly during baking), then transfer to a baking rack and let cool.

1 large egg
8 tablespoons (1 stick) unsalted butter, softened
¼ cup firmly packed dark brown sugar
¼ teaspoon vanilla extract
¾ cup brown rice flour
½ cup cornstarch
Pinch of fine sea salt
¾ cup (3 ounces) hazelnuts, finely chopped
⅓ cup raspberry jam

:: **Makes about 30**

almond jam
sandwich cookies

1 cup (4 ounces)
blanched, slivered
almonds
¼ cup cornstarch
8 tablespoons (1 stick)
unsalted butter,
softened
⅓ cup sugar
1 large egg yolk
½ teaspoon almond
extract
1 cup brown rice flour
Pinch of fine sea salt
½ cup berry or apricot
jam, or ¼ cup of each
Confectioners' sugar

:: **Makes 16**

A PERENNIAL FAVORITE, THIS version is more delicate than the usual jam-filled cookie. Be sure to choose jam without large chunks of fruit in it (raspberry and sieved apricot are good) or the top cookies may break when you press them down. Naturally, you can also make flat cookies with this dough, in which case roll it ¼ inch thick, and bake the cookies for about 12 minutes.

1. Preheat the oven to 400°F. Line two large baking sheets with parchment paper. (If using only one baking sheet, cool under running water and dry before reusing, as it must be cold.)

2. Combine the almonds and cornstarch in a food processor, and grind to a fine meal. Set aside. Add the butter and sugar to the processor, and blend until creamy. Add the egg yolk and almond extract, and blend until smooth. Add the rice flour, salt, and the almond mixture, and process briefly until a rough ball of dough forms.

3. Turn the dough out onto a sheet of plastic wrap. Press together into a disk, cut in half, and set one-half aside. Cover the remaining half with a second sheet of plastic wrap, and roll out ⅛ inch thick. Cut out as many 2½-inch rounds as possible, rerolling the trimmings for more cookies. Transfer to one of the baking sheets. Repeat with the remaining dough, and cut a ½-inch circle from the center of each one after transferring the cookies to the second baking sheet. Reroll the trimmings, making an equal number of whole and ring cookies. Bake until just starting to brown at the edges, 10 minutes. Transfer to wire racks and let cool.

4. Center a generous teaspoon of jam on each solid cookie, spreading it out a little. Top with the rings, pressing down very lightly. Dust with confectioners' sugar.

teff brownies

12 tablespoons (1½
   sticks) unsalted butter,
   cut up
5 ounces 60% to 70%
   dark chocolate,
   chopped
1 ounce unsweetened
   chocolate, chopped
3 large eggs
1 cup sugar
1 teaspoon vanilla
   extract
¾ cup dark teff flour
¼ teaspoon salt
1 cup (4 ounces)
   walnuts, chopped
Confectioners' sugar

:: **Makes 16**

IF THERE WERE NO other reason for buying teff flour, these spectacular, trufflelike brownies would be cause enough.

1. Preheat the oven to 350°F. Line an 8-inch square cake pan with parchment paper.

2. Combine the butter, dark chocolate, and unsweetened chocolate in the top of a double boiler. Melt over barely simmering water, and let cool to lukewarm. Beat the eggs, sugar, and vanilla until well combined. Beat in the chocolate mixture, then the teff flour and salt. Stir in the walnuts.

3. Transfer the batter to the prepared pan, and smooth the top. Bake until the top is set and pale brown but the interior is still moist, about 35 minutes. An inserted toothpick should emerge slightly sticky. The brownies will continue to cook for a few minutes as they cool. Let cool completely in the pan. Unmold, and trim off the crisp edges (nibbling on these bits is the cook's privilege), so that when cut, every brownie will be fudgy. Dust with confectioners' sugar. Cut into 16 squares.

Teff: The Lost Grain of Ethiopia ::

The ancient North African land of Ethiopia lies below Egypt. Ringed by mountains, the high central plateau is between seven and ten thousand feet above sea level. Happily, the principal cereal crop is a hardy plant that manages to thrive at this altitude. Teff has seeds so small that the name means "lost," but there are lots of seeds per plant. When ground, they make a high-protein flour that's used for the national bread, injera. To make it, Ethiopian women mix teff flour with water and allow the batter to ferment for up to three days when it is poured onto a huge griddle and cooked on one side only, the result is a thin, 30-inch pancake laced with a million tiny holes. Cooks drape several of these moist, chewy, sour crêpes over a shallow basket so diners can tear off pieces and use them as scoops for the spicy stews of the region. Don't expect traditional injera at Ethiopian restaurants in North America; most of them use Aunt Jemima pancake mix.

Although teff is indigenous to Ethiopia, farmers in other parts of the world grow it as a cereal crop. The seed heads are so tiny—smaller than pinheads—that teff is sold complete with germ and bran, whether left whole or ground into flour. Teff grown in the United States shows protein levels of as much as 15 percent (higher than nearly all other cereals, including wheat) and has the highest calcium content of any grain. High in fiber, the protein it contains is a plant version of albumin, the protein found in egg white. It comes in two nutritionally identical varieties, light and dark. Ivory teff flour has a mellow, nutty flavor; the brown kind does too, but has attractive, unexpected chocolate overtones.

Teff is sold in natural foods stores and by mail order. You can also buy it direct from Wayne and Elisabeth Carlson of the Teff Company (see page 212), who cultivate teff in southwestern Idaho. Wayne worked as a biologist in Ethiopia for some years, hence his interest in this amazing grain. The crop thrives in volcanic soil on the Idaho-Oregon border, which is watered by melted-snow runoff, and the Carlsons have progressed from growing a few rows of teff in their backyard to harvesting, threshing, milling, and packaging tons of teff seed annually. Not forgetting its land of origin, they return a portion of the supergrains they have developed to Ethiopia for agricultural trials each year. They also donate seed to a relief agency for planting in Ethiopia.

teff-peanut butter fudge cookies

3/4 cup dark or light teff flour

3/4 cup brown rice flour, plus additional for forming cookies

6 tablespoons sugar

1/2 teaspoon fine sea salt

1/2 teaspoon xanthan gum

4 tablespoons (1/2 stick) unsalted butter, cold, cut into small cubes

2 tablespoons canola oil

1 cup smooth or chunky peanut butter

1 large egg

1 teaspoon vanilla extract

:: **Makes about 36**

REMINISCENT OF SLIGHTLY GRANULAR, old-fashioned fudge, these satisfying, soft cookies are quickly mixed in a food processor.

1. Preheat the oven to 350°F. Line two large baking sheets with parchment paper. (If using only one baking sheet, cool under running water and dry before reusing, as it must be cold.)

2. Combine the teff flour, rice flour, sugar, salt, xanthan gum, and butter in a food processor. Process briefly to form a fine meal. Add the canola oil, peanut butter, egg, and vanilla, and pulse on and off until a soft dough forms. Pinch off pieces the size of a walnut, compress slightly, and roll into balls. Flatten slightly into 1½ inches × ½-inch-thick disks. Arrange on the baking sheets about 1 inch apart. Using a fork dipped in rice flour, flatten the cookies a bit more while forming a crisscross pattern on each one. Bake, one sheet at a time, until the cookies are lightly browned, 15 minutes. Let cool in the pan for 5 minutes, then transfer to a wire rack to cool completely.

teff gingerbread with dates

THE FLAVOR AND TEXTURE of this dense and sticky gingerbread is irresistible. Adding dates is probably gilding the lily, but they make a good thing even better.

1. Heat the oven to 350°F. Line an 8-inch square cake pan with parchment paper.

2. Combine ¾ cup of the teff flour with the rice flour, cornstarch, baking soda, baking powder, salt, xanthan gum, cloves, cinnamon, and ginger, and set aside.

3. In a separate bowl, beat the butter and sugar until light and fluffy, then beat in the egg. Add the molasses and ½ cup hot water, and beat until smooth, about 30 seconds. Beat in the flour mixture. Toss the dates with the remaining teaspoon teff flour, to prevent them from sticking together, and stir in. Pour the batter into the prepared pan. Bake until firm and an inserted toothpick comes out clean, about 30 minutes. Let cool completely in the pan before turning out. Dust with confectioners' sugar. Cut in half, and then cut each half into 4 or 5 bars.

¾ cup plus 1 teaspoon dark teff flour
⅓ cup brown rice flour
¼ cup cornstarch
1 teaspoon baking soda
1 teaspoon baking powder
Pinch of fine sea salt
½ teaspoon xanthan gum
¼ teaspoon ground cloves
¼ teaspoon ground cinnamon
2 teaspoons ground ginger
1 stick (4 ounces) unsalted butter, softened
½ cup sugar
1 large egg
½ cup dark molasses
4 Medjool dates, pitted and chopped
Confectioners' sugar

:: Serves 8 to 10

rice flour gingerbread cows

1 cup brown rice flour, plus extra for rolling cookies

1 cup cornstarch

½ teaspoon fine sea salt

¼ teaspoon xanthan gum

½ teaspoon baking soda

1 teaspoon ground ginger

½ teaspoon ground cinnamon

¼ teaspoon ground cloves

½ cup dark molasses

¼ cup sugar

3 tablespoons unsalted butter

:: **Makes 24, approximately 2½ by 3½ inches each**

I LIVE IN NORTHERN California, so I make gingerbread cows every holiday season instead of snowmen, and hang some of them on the Christmas tree. (One memorable year, a friend's basset hound thought this was a super idea, so now I place them higher up.) These crisp, German-style cookies can be left plain or decorated with frosting, and of course you can use any kind of cookie cutter you like. If you want to utilize your gingerbread cookies as tree decorations, make a hole in each one with a skewer before baking, and thread with ribbon after they cool.

1. Preheat the oven to 350°F. Line two large baking sheets with parchment paper. (If using only one baking sheet, cool under running water and dry before reusing, as it must be cold.)

2. Mix the rice flour and cornstarch with the salt, xanthan gum, baking soda, ginger, cinnamon, and cloves.

3. Heat the molasses to the boiling point in a medium saucepan over medium heat, and stir in the sugar and butter. Remove from the heat. Stir in

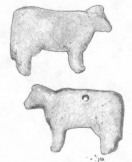

the flour mixture one-third at a time, along with 1 to 2 tablespoons water, if needed, to make a workable dough. Turn out onto a lightly rice-floured surface and knead a few times until silky smooth. Cut the ball of dough in half and work with one section at a time.

4. Dusting the dough lightly with rice flour, roll out $\frac{1}{4}$ inch thick. Using a rice-floured cookie cutter, cut out as many gingerbread figures as possible, rerolling the trimmings to make more. (It's easiest to lift away the excess dough from around the cookies, and then transfer them to the baking sheet on a metal spatula.) Bake until the cookies puff up slightly and lighten to a tan color, 6 to 7 minutes. Let cool on the baking sheet for 5 minutes, then place on a wire rack. Repeat with the remaining dough. If decorating with frosting, let the cookies cool completely first.

rice flour vanilla wafers

6 tablespoons
   (¾ stick) unsalted
   butter, softened
¼ cup sugar
1 large egg
½ teaspoon vanilla
   extract
½ cup cornstarch
¼ cup brown rice flour
Pinch of fine sea salt
½ teaspoon xanthan
   gum

:: Makes about 30

SERVE THESE CRISPY MINIATURE wafers with any creamy dessert, including French Chocolate Mousse (page 206), or Quick Mango Sorbet (page 207). You can also sandwich them together with melted dark chocolate, and enjoy with a cup of coffee.

1. Preheat the oven to 375°F. Line a baking sheet with parchment paper, and fit a pastry bag with a ⅜-inch plain round metal tip.

2. Cream the butter and sugar together until smooth, then beat in the egg and vanilla. Sift the cornstarch, rice flour, salt, and xanthan gum over the bowl, and fold in. Transfer to the pastry bag, and pipe out 1-inch blobs, 1 inch apart, on the baking sheet. Flatten each cookie gently with the back of a spoon dipped in water to prevent sticking. Bake until the cookies are tinged golden brown around the edges, 10 minutes. Let cool on a rack.

pine nut wafers

BASED ON A POPULAR Italian cookie, these airy, delicate wafers go perfectly with espresso or ice cream. Pine nuts (pignoli) can be found in natural foods stores and Italian groceries.

1. Preheat the oven to 350°F. Line two large baking sheets with parchment paper. (If using only one baking sheet, cool under running water and dry before reusing, as it must be cold.)

2. Beat the eggs until well combined, 20 seconds, then gradually add the sugar. Continue beating to the ribbon stage, about 7 minutes. Place a fine sieve over the bowl, and add the rice flour and cornstarch. Shake over the mixture, and fold in. Add the lemon zest, and fold in.

3. Working with half the batter at a time, drop by teaspoonfuls onto a baking sheet, leaving 1 inch spaces between them. Top each cookie with 4 or 5 pine nuts. Bake until pale gold, 12 to 15 minutes. Prepare the second batch while the first batch bakes. Leave the cookies on the baking sheets for 5 minutes before transferring them to a wire rack to cool completely.

2 large eggs
½ cup sugar
½ cup brown rice flour
½ cup cornstarch
Grated zest of 1 small lemon
3 to 4 tablespoons pine nuts

:: Makes about 30

Tarts and Pies

DON'T BE AFRAID OF MAKING a piecrust. Armed with a food processor, a roll of plastic wrap, and a rolling pin, anyone can do it. And even experienced cooks (not to mention experienced eaters) are amazed by the tender qualities of pastry made with rice flour. There are two secrets. One is rolling the dough out between two sheets of plastic wrap, which not only keeps warm hands off it but avoids adding extra flour, which makes any pastry cardboard-y. The other secret is making sure that your creation is enjoyed soon after baking, so that the filling contrasts with the crisp pastry. The only exceptions are tarts filled with chopped or ground-nut mixtures, which will keep for two or three days without softening. Double-crust pies made with gluten-free pastry are also easy to achieve—I've included an apple pie, but you can use any fruit you like.

rice flour tart shell

THESE INSTRUCTIONS LOOK LENGTHY, but the actual process is quick. Set out everything you need beforehand except the butter, which should be taken out of the refrigerator just before you use it. If you plan to make a savory quiche or tart, omit the sugar. This pastry is more fragile than the wheat-flour variety, with a delectable crunch. The dough (or the semibaked shells) can be frozen.

1 1/2 cups brown rice flour
1/2 cup cornstarch
1/4 teaspoon xanthan gum
1/4 teaspoon fine sea salt
1 tablespoon sugar (omit for savory tarts or quiches)
12 tablespoons (1 1/2 sticks) unsalted butter, cold, cut in small cubes
1 large egg

1. Combine the rice flour, cornstarch, xanthan gum, salt, and sugar in a food processor. Process briefly to mix. Add the butter, and pulse until it forms pea-sized lumps. Add the egg, and process briefly to mix. Add a tablespoon of ice water, and pulse 5 or 6 times to make a ball of dough that barely clings together.

2. Turn the dough out, crumbs and all, and form into a log with your cupped hands. Cut off about half the dough (wrap and refrigerate the remainder), and place on a sheet of plastic wrap. Top with a second sheet of plastic wrap, and roll out 1/8 inch thick, forming a 10- or 11-inch circle. (It should be 2 inches wider than the tart pan you plan to use.) If the edges look rough, lift the top sheet of plastic wrap, tuck them in, then roll lightly to incorporate. Turn the pastry over to check for an even thickness.

⁞ Makes two 8-inch pastry shells, or one 8-inch and one 9-inch shell

3. Peel off the top layer of plastic wrap, and flop the dough into the tart pan. Remove the second layer of plastic wrap. (If it sticks, place the pan, plastic and all, on a cookie sheet and refrigerate for 10 minutes.) Ease the dough against the sides without stretching it, making a little pouch on the inside rim. This way, the edge of the tart shell will be thicker. Push the dough against the fluted sides and trim even with the top of the pan. If there are any holes or thin places, just patch with the trimmings. Prick a few holes in the base. Secure the pastry rim by pushing it very slightly over the top of the pan (see below). Place the pan in the freezer for 10 minutes. Wrap and refrigerate any dough trimmings in case you need them for patching later.

4. Preheat the oven to 350°F.

5. Bake the shell for 15 minutes until firm and just starting to color. Supporting the pan from underneath so the ring doesn't come loose, transfer to a rack and let cool before filling. For a fully cooked shell, bake for 30 minutes.

PREBAKING A TART SHELL

To help make sure that a pastry shell remains crisp in relation to the filling, it should be prebaked just until firm but not colored. However, baking an empty shell has its perils: the sides slump and the base puffs up. Most recipes suggest lining it with a sheet of aluminum foil and dried beans, but this risks tearing the tender pastry when you lift the foil. Professional pastry chefs have a better method: they just press the pastry up and very slightly over the sides so that a $\frac{1}{16}$-inch lip of pastry rests on top of the rim, which anchors it. (Don't make this too extreme or the baked shell might break when you unmold it.) Freeze the shell for 10 minutes before baking. Check after 5 minutes of baking time. If the base has ballooned—it usually doesn't—quickly deflate with a knife tip.

Prebaked Tart Shell First Aid

If a prebaked pastry shell should develop cracks as it bakes, usually the result of stretching the dough, don't panic. Hairline cracks don't matter, but wider ones would let the filling escape. Let the shell cool, then simply roll small pieces of leftover, room temperature raw pastry dough into little ropes and gently smooth them in position, or form a larger, flat patch for a cracked rim. Then fill the tart and bake it. No one will ever know.

pecan tart

9-inch Rice Flour Tart Shell (page 169), half baked and cooled

4 tablespoons apricot jam, heated, sieved, and cooled slightly

1 cup (4 ounces) pecans, plus 12 halves for decoration

½ cup sugar

6 tablespoons (¾ stick) unsalted butter, softened

2 large eggs

1 tablespoon dark rum

2 tablespoons brown rice flour

:: Serves 10

TRADITIONAL INGREDIENTS USED IN a different way turn this tart into an elegant finale for a holiday meal. Unlike creamy or fruit-filled tarts, it will keep for two or three days in the refrigerator without the pastry shell losing its tender crispness. If you want to make a good thing even better, bake the tart without the pecan decoration, let cool, cover with the dark chocolate glaze used on the Chocolate Éclairs (page 196), arrange the pecan halves on top, and let stand until set.

1. Preheat the oven to 350°F.

2. Set the tart shell, still in the pan, on a baking sheet. Spread the jam gently over the base, using the back of a spoon.

3. Combine the pecans and sugar in a food processor, and process to a fine meal. Add the butter, and process to blend. Add the eggs and rum, and process until smooth. Add the rice flour, and process just long enough to mix. Using a rubber spatula, spread in the tart shell on top of the jam and arrange the pecan halves around the edge, like the numerals on a clock. Bake until the surface is golden and the pastry is golden brown, about 35 minutes. Place the pan on a wire rack and let cool. Unmold, and transfer the tart to a flat platter.

Unmolding a Tart from a Loose-Based Tart or Quiche Pan

Set the cooled tart pan over an unopened can and let the fluted rim fall down. The tart can then be transferred, still on the base, to a platter. Alternatively, carefully slide the flat base from a second tart pan between the pastry and the base of the pan it was baked in, and transfer the tart to a flat platter. (Most metal spatulas are too narrow for adequate support.)

almond-raspberry tart

9-inch Rice Flour Tart
Shell (page 169), half
baked and cooled

1/3 cup raspberry jam,
heated

1 cup (4 ounces) whole
almonds

1/2 cup sugar

8 tablespoons (1 stick)
unsalted butter,
softened

2 large eggs

2 tablespoons white rice
flour

GLAZES

1/2 cup apricot jam,
heated and sieved

1 cup confectioners'
sugar, sifted

2 to 3 tablespoons
lemon juice

:: **Serves 10**

TWO GLAZES—APRICOT AND LEMON—
TOP this scrumptious tart, which is claimed by
the Swedes as an Alexandertorte, and by the English as a Bakewell Tart. Unlike creamy, filled
tarts, this one will keep refrigerated for three
days without losing its crispness.

1. Preheat the oven to 350°F.

2. Set the tart shell, still in the pan, on a baking sheet.
Spread the jam gently over the base, using the back of a
spoon.

3. Combine the almonds and sugar in a food processor,
and process to a fine meal. Add the butter, and process
to blend. Add the eggs, and process until smooth. Add
the rice flour, and process just long enough to mix.

4. Using a rubber spatula, spread the almond mixture
on top of the jam and smooth the surface. Bake until the
filling is golden and slightly domed, about 35 minutes. An
inserted toothpick should emerge clean. Place the pan
on a wire rack, and let the tart cool before unmolding.
Transfer to a flat platter.

5. Brush the surface of the tart with the apricot glaze and
let set, about 1 hour. Stir the confectioners' sugar with
just enough lemon juice to make a runny frosting, and
brush or drizzle on top.

raisin-walnut tart

BASED ON AN OLD Scottish recipe, the rich fruit filling is balanced by a splash of raspberry vinegar. The tart will hold well, refrigerated, for three days. Should it last that long, which is unlikely. It also freezes well.

1. Heat the oven to 350°F. Set the tart shell, still in the pan, on a baking sheet.

2. Combine the brown sugar, butter, vinegar, and egg, and mix well. Stir in the raisins and dried fruit, and add the walnuts. Spoon evenly into the pastry shell. Bake until the pastry is golden and the filling is firm, about 30 minutes.

3. Place the pan on a wire rack, and let the tart cool before unmolding. Transfer to a flat platter. Dust lightly with confectioners' sugar.

8-inch Rice Flour Tart Shell (page 169), half baked and cooled

6 tablespoons packed dark brown sugar

4 tablespoons (½ stick) unsalted butter, melted and cooled to lukewarm

1 tablespoon raspberry vinegar or other mellow red wine vinegar

1 large egg

½ cup raisins

¾ cup mixed dried fruit (currants, whole dried cherries, chopped pitted prunes)

½ cup chopped walnuts

Confectioners' sugar

∷ **Serves 6 to 8**

nut crumb crust

1½ cups (6 ounces)
   almonds
2 tablespoons sugar
½ cup brown rice flour
¼ teaspoon allspice
8 tablespoons (1 stick)
   unsalted butter, cold,
   cut up

Makes one 9-inch piecrust

THIS SIMPLE CRUST, WHICH you can pat into a pie pan or roll out, also makes a good base for a cheesecake.

1. Preheat the oven to 325°F. Have ready a 9-inch glass pie pan.

2. Combine the almonds, sugar, rice flour, and allspice in a food processor. Process to a fine meal. Add the butter, and process briefly until coarse crumbs form.

3. Either press the crumbs into the pie pan with your fingers or, for a neater result, roll between two sheets of plastic wrap into a 10-inch circle. Pick up the top sheet and fold the rough edges inward, then replace the plastic wrap and roll again to make a circle with a smooth edge. Peel off the top sheet of wrap, invert the pie pan over the crust, and turn the whole thing right side up. Remove the remaining plastic wrap, and repair any problem areas with your fingers. Bake until firm and a golden-tan color, about 20 minutes. Let cool before filling.

strawberry-cream cheese tart

THE CHARM OF a good berry tart lies in the contrast of crisp pastry and luscious filling. To be at its best, it should be enjoyed within a couple of hours of being made, except for the pastry shell, which you can bake ahead. Be sure to choose small, sweet, aromatic strawberries, not the hard, tasteless ones with white centers so beloved by supermarkets for their shipping qualities and long shelf life.

1. Leave the tart shell in the pie pan, for support. Brush the base of the tart shell with 2 tablespoons of the currant jelly.

2. Combine the cream cheese, yogurt, and lemon curd in a food processor, and blend until smooth. Spoon over the jelly, and smooth the surface. Top with the strawberries, and glaze them with the remaining 2 tablespoons currant jelly.

3. Refrigerate for 30 minutes or up to 2 hours. Unmold, transfer to a flat platter, and scatter with sliced almonds, if using.

GREEK YOGURT

Authentic Greek yogurt is made from whole milk and is drained of whey, leaving it as thick as sour cream.

9-inch Nut Crumb Crust, fully baked (page 176) and cooled

4 tablespoons red currant jelly, melted

½ pound fresh cream cheese

6 tablespoons thick Greek yogurt (see below)

2 tablespoons all-butter lemon curd

1 pint small, ripe strawberries, preferably organic, halved

2 tablespoons sliced almonds, lightly toasted, optional

.: Serves 8 to 10

Total is the brand most readily available. To make your own, line a colander with several layers of dampened cheesecloth and place over a bowl. Add a 32-ounce tub of plain whole milk (preferably cream-top) yogurt and let drip overnight, refrigerated. Makes about 3 cups.

rice flour pasta frolla

ITALIAN SWEET SHORTCRUST PASTRY, or pasta frolla, is exceptionally tender. It's easy to make in a food processor, but should it start to become sticky while being rolled, just pop the dough, pan and all, into the refrigerator for 10 minutes, then continue where you left off.

Combine the rice flour, cornstarch, xanthan gum, baking powder, sugar, salt, butter, and lemon zest, if using, in a food processor. Process briefly until the mixture resembles coarse meal. Add the eggs and 1 tablespoon cold water, and process just long enough to combine into a rough ball. Turn out onto a sheet of plastic wrap, crumbs and all, and push together into a log. Cut into 3 equal pieces (or according to instructions for Ricotta Tart, page 180), enclose in plastic wrap, and refrigerate for 1 hour or up to 24 hours.

1½ cups brown rice flour
½ cup cornstarch
½ teaspoon xanthan gum
½ teaspoon baking powder
¼ cup sugar
Pinch of fine sea salt
8 tablespoons (1 stick) unsalted butter, cold, cut up
½ teaspoon grated lemon zest, optional
2 large eggs lightly beaten

:: Makes three 8-inch tart shells or the base and lattice top for Ricotta Tart, page 180

ricotta tart

1 recipe Rice Flour Pasta
Frolla (page 179)
1½ pounds ricotta,
preferably whole milk
½ cup sugar
4 large eggs
1 tablespoon Marsala or
dark rum
1 teaspoon vanilla
extract
1 tablespoon brown rice
flour
2 tablespoons Candied
Orange Peel (page
182) or store-bought,
diced
Grated zest of 1 small
orange
4 tablespoons golden
raisins
2 tablespoons pine nuts

∷ **Serves 10**

PERHAPS EVEN MORE ADDICTIVE than a New York–style cheesecake, this dessert is based on a very old Roman specialty. Creamy but not cloying, it's hard to resist seconds.

1. Preheat the oven to 350°F. Butter a 9-inch springform pan.

2. Unwrap the dough and cut off one-third for the lattice top. Place it between 2 sheets of plastic wrap, roll into a 10 × 8-inch rectangle, and refrigerate, flat.

3. Place the remaining dough between 2 sheets of plastic wrap and roll into a 14-inch circle. Peel off the top sheet of plastic wrap and flop the dough into the pan. Remove the second sheet of plastic wrap, ease the dough against the bottom and sides of the pan without stretching it, and trim even with the top.

4. In a large bowl, stir together the ricotta and sugar. Beat in 3 whole eggs and 1 egg white (reserve the yolk), one at a time. Stir in the Marsala, vanilla, rice flour, candied orange peel, orange zest, and raisins. Pour the mixture into the crust. Scatter the pine nuts evenly on top.

5. Cut the reserved pastry into ten ½-inch-wide strips. Form a lattice on top of the filling, trimming to fit. Using a knife blade to loosen it from the pan first, fold the excess pastry down to cover the edges of the lattice. Blend the reserved egg yolk with 1 teaspoon water, and brush the pastry surfaces with it. Bake until the crust browns and the filling is set, 45 minutes. Let stand for 5 minutes. Loosen the sides of the tart with a knife blade, then release the pan rim. Transfer to a wire rack, still on the base, and let cool. Loosen the bottom crust from the pan base with a wide metal spatula, and slide the tart onto a flat serving platter. Serve at room temperature.

candied orange peel

6 oranges
2 cups (1 pound) sugar,
  plus additional for
  coating

FOR SOME REASON, CANDIED orange peel seems to be available in grocery stores only during the holiday season. The supermarket kind isn't worth buying, and the imported or European-style variety, though delicious, is wildly expensive. The alternative is to make your own. Invaluable for baking, it can also be turned into a delightful after-dinner candy. Simply half dip the sugar-coated strips in melted dark chocolate, and let set.

:: Makes about 2 cups

1. Cut a small slice off the top and bottom of each orange. Make four vertical cuts, through the peel only, at equal intervals. Pull off the peel in four quarters, reserving the fruit for another use.

2. Place the peel in a pan, and cover with cold water. Bring to a boil and then drain. Repeat twice more, to leach out any bitterness. When cool enough to handle, pare off a little of the white pith if it is very thick, but do not remove it all or the peel will harden when candied. Cut each section in half lengthways.

3. Combine the sugar with 2 cups cold water in a heavy pan, and bring to a boil. Simmer for 5 minutes, then add the peel. Simmer gently for 1 hour, and let cool in the syrup. Remove the peel and cut into ¼-inch-wide strips. Let dry overnight on a wire rack set over a sheet of aluminum foil to catch the drips. Cover a plate with sugar, and roll the strips in it. Let dry out for a few more hours on a clean, dry wire rack. Place in an airtight container, and store in the refrigerator or freezer.

rich cornmeal piecrust

½ cup cornmeal, preferably stone ground

1 cup sweet white rice flour

½ cup cornstarch

¼ cup sugar

¼ teaspoon xanthan gum

¼ teaspoon fine sea salt

12 tablespoons (1½ sticks) unsalted butter, cold, cut in small cubes

1 large egg

:: **Makes one 9-inch double crust pie shell or two open-faced pie shells**

SO CRUNCHY AND DELECTABLE that you can make cookies with it, this piecrust provides just the right contrast for the tender fruit filling. As regular cornmeal is on the coarse side, I whirl it in a food processor for 2 minutes to get a finer texture. To make cornmeal cookies, roll the dough ¼ inch thick, and cut them out with a 2½-inch cutter. Brush the cookies with cream or milk, and sprinkle with sugar before baking at 350°F until golden brown at the edges, about 15 minutes.

Process the cornmeal in a food processor for 2 minutes until more finely ground. Add the rice flour, cornstarch, sugar, xanthan gum, and salt, and process to combine. Add the butter, and pulse until it forms pea-sized lumps. Add the egg, and process briefly to mix. Add 1 tablespoon ice water, and process briefly to make a ball of dough that barely clings together, adding another teaspoon of water if necessary to make a damp dough. Turn the dough out, crumbs and all, onto a sheet of plastic wrap, and form into a log with your cupped hands. Cut in half. The dough is now ready to use or can be enclosed in plastic wrap and refrigerated for up to 24 hours.

apple pie with a rich cornmeal crust

IF YOU HANKER AFTER a double-crust pie, here's how to make one with a tempting gluten-free crust. Naturally, you can substitute 5 cups of any fruit filling you please, but shorten the baking time a little for soft summer fruits.

1. Preheat the oven to 425°F. Have ready a 9-inch pie pan, preferably a heavy aluminum one with a pierced base so steam can escape, which helps the texture of the bottom crust. Combine the apples, lemon zest and juice, raisins, ⅓ cup of the sugar, rice flour, and cinnamon, toss to mix well, and set aside.

2. Working with half the dough at a time, roll out between sheets of plastic wrap, lifting the top sheet and tucking in the rough edges, into 11-inch circles. Set one circle aside for the top crust. Use the other circle to line the pie pan: peel off the top sheet of plastic wrap and flop the dough into place, then carefully peel off the remaining sheet. Add the fruit, piling it up slightly, and dot with the butter. Cover with the top crust, seal the rim by fluting, or pressing with the tines of a fork, and trim off any excess dough. Combine the egg yolk with 1 teaspoon water, and brush over the top, but not the rim, as it might get too brown. Sprinkle with the remaining tablespoon of sugar. Cut a few slits in the top for steam to escape. Place the pie pan on a baking sheet, to catch any spills. Bake for

5 or 6 Fuji or Braeburn apples, peeled, cored, halved, and cut into ⅛-inch-thick slices (to make 5 cups)
Grated zest of ½ lemon
2 tablespoons lemon juice
½ cup golden raisins
⅓ cup plus 1 tablespoon sugar
3 tablespoons white rice flour
¼ teaspoon ground cinnamon
Pastry for Rich Cornmeal Piecrust (page 184)
2 tablespoons unsalted butter, cut into small cubes
1 egg yolk

Serves 8 to 10

20 minutes, then reduce the heat to 350°F and continue baking until the filling is tender when pierced with a narrow knife blade through one of the slits, and the crust is golden brown, about 30 minutes more. (Keep checking as it bakes, and if the top brown too fast, cover lightly with a sheet of aluminum foil.) Serve warm, not hot.

Cakes and Desserts

ONE OF THE MANY REWARDS inherent in being a wheat-free cook is that your cakes are much lighter than anybody else's. (Hint: professional pastry chefs choose low-gluten cake flour for a reason; using no-gluten flour goes one better.) And thanks to using nut flours, and eggs to make them rise as opposed to lots of baking powder, the cakes here even offer some good nutrition along with their enticing flavors and textures. Furthermore, since many of the premium quality ingredients are naturally sweet, you can get away with using far less sugar than usual.

four-ingredient chocolate-walnut cake

THIS FOUR-INGREDIENT CHOCOLATE CAKE (or five, if you count a dusting of powdered sugar) tastes sinfully rich, but contains no wheat flour, no egg yolks, no butter . . . and no cholesterol.

2½ cups (10 ounces) walnuts

4 tablespoons unsweetened natural cocoa powder (not Dutch-processed)

9 tablespoons Eggbeaters or other liquid egg substitute

1 cup sugar

Confectioners' sugar, optional

1. Preheat the oven to 350°F. Grease the sides of an 8-inch round cake pan with a mild-tasting vegetable oil, and line the base with a circle of parchment paper.

2. Combine the walnuts and cocoa powder in a food processor. Pulse on and off to form a mealy consistency, stopping when the mixture starts to climb the sides of the bowl and threatens to become a paste.

3. Using an electric mixer, beat the Eggbeaters for 30 seconds, then slowly add the sugar. Beat until the mixture triples and readies the ribbon stage, about 3 minutes. (Eggbeaters thicken more quickly than whole eggs.) Fold in the walnut mixture in three batches, spooning it around the edge of the bowl. (This helps to avoid deflating the batter.)

4. Transfer the batter to the pan, and smooth the top. Bake until the cake resists a light finger pressure and shrinks away slightly from the

:: **Serves 8**

sides of the pan, 25 to 30 minutes. An inserted toothpick should come out slightly sticky. Do not overbake, as this would make the cake dry. Let stand for 10 minutes, then turn out onto a cooling rack. The cake is meant to be quite low. Peel off the paper, turn the cake right side up on a second rack, and let cool. Dust with confectioners' sugar, if using, and transfer to a flat platter.

Cake Pan Credentials

For the best baking results, use professional-quality, heavy-gauge aluminum cake pans with 2-inch-deep sides and a 6-cup capacity. Made for bakery use and available through top kitchenware stores such as Williams-Sonoma, they bake evenly and hold more than the flimsy, too-shallow kind, which promote uneven rising, scorching, and overflows. (As a general rule, never fill a cake pan more than two-thirds full.) Lining a cake pan with parchment aids in getting the cake out safely, and helps to prevent overbrowning the underside.

chocolate-hazelnut truffle cake

HAZELNUTS AND DARK CHOCOLATE, a favorite combination in Italian confectionery, puts this fudgy torta into the deluxe class.

1. Preheat the oven to 350°F. Butter the sides of an 8-inch round cake pan and line the base with parchment paper.

2. Combine the hazelnuts, chocolate, 2 tablespoons of the sugar, the rice flour, and cocoa powder in a food processor. Process to make a fine meal of even consistency. Add the orange zest.

3. Combine the eggs and the remaining sugar in a large bowl, and beat until the mixture reaches the ribbon stage, about 7 minutes. Using a rubber spatula, spoon the hazelnut-chocolate mixture around the edge of the bowl and fold in, deflating the batter as little as possible. Transfer to the pan. Bake until the cake resists a light finger pressure and starts to pull away from the sides of the pan, 22 to 25 minutes. Do not overbake or the cake will be dry instead of slightly fudgy. Let the cake cool in the pan for 10 minutes, then run a knife blade around the sides to loosen it. Unmold and gently peel off the parchment. Let cool, right side up, on a rack. Dust lightly with cocoa powder before serving.

1 cup (4 ounces) hazelnuts

3 ounces 60% to 70% dark chocolate, finely chopped, or ½ cup 60% chocolate chips

⅓ cup sugar

2 tablespoons brown rice flour

1 tablespoon unsweetened natural cocoa powder (not Dutch-processed), plus extra for dusting top of cake

1 teaspoon grated orange zest

3 large eggs

Cocoa powder

:: Serves 8 to 10

Cheating with Chocolate

Ghirardelli, a fine old company based in San Francisco, makes excellent dark chocolate with 60 percent cacao butter for a reasonable price. If you can't find it, and don't feel like paying a premium for imported dark chocolate, use regular dark baker's chocolate in a ratio of three parts baker's chocolate to one part unsweetened baker's chocolate. This will raise the cacao-butter content and give a richer flavor and a smoother texture to chocolate cakes and glazes.

extra-light chocolate cake

REMINISCENT OF ANGEL FOOD cake in texture but a trifle more substantial, this lofty cake contains a dash of espresso for a subtle mocha flavor.

1. Preheat the oven to 350°F. Have ready a 10-inch tube pan, ungreased.
2. Combine the cornstarch, cocoa powder, cinnamon, and salt, and set aside.
3. Separate the eggs into 2 large bowls. Beat the egg whites until frothy. Slowly add ½ cup of the sugar and beat at high speed until stiff but not dry.
4. Using the same beaters (no need to wash them), beat the remaining ¾ cup sugar into the egg yolks a little at a time, and beat until the mixture is very thick and a pale lemon color, about 5 minutes. Beat in the dissolved coffee. Sift the cornstarch-cocoa mixture on top, and fold in lightly but thoroughly. Fold the beaten egg whites into the batter. Spoon into the tube pan, and rap it smartly on the counter to banish any air pockets. Bake until the cake springs back from a light finger touch, 50 minutes. Invert the pan (with the tube resting over a bottle if the pan does not have feet), and let cool. When cold, loosen the sides and center of the cake with a sharp knife blade, and unmold with the base of the cake facing upward. Dust with confectioners' sugar just before serving.

½ cup cornstarch
¼ cup unsweetened natural cocoa powder (not Dutch-processed)
½ teaspoon ground cinnamon
Pinch of fine sea salt
6 large eggs
1¼ cups sugar
1 tablespoon instant espresso (or regular) coffee, dissolved in 1 tablespoon dark rum or water
Confectioners' sugar

:: **Serves 10 to 12**

chocolate-glazed
chestnut gateau

½ cup chestnut flour or
  brown rice flour
¼ cup cornstarch
1 teaspoon baking
  powder
4 large eggs, separated
¾ cup sugar
1 teaspoon vanilla extract

FILLING
1 can (8½ ounces)
  sweetened chestnut
  spread, such as
  Clément Faugier
4 tablespoons (½
  stick) unsalted butter,
  softened
1 tablespoon dark rum

GLAZE
½ cup apricot jam,
  heated and sieved
4 ounces 60% to
  70% dark chocolate,
  chopped
2 tablespoons canola oil

:: Serves 10

A FRENCH-INSPIRED WINTER FESTIVAL cake that unites light sponge cake with a rich, creamy chestnut filling and a dark chocolate glaze. On trying it, one guest said in surprise, "I've never liked chestnut *anything*, but this is delicious," and happily accepted a second slice. (Just to make sure that his taste buds were not deceiving him, of course.)

1. Preheat the oven to 350°F. Butter the sides of two 8-inch cake pans, and line the bottoms with parchment paper.
2. Sift together the chestnut flour, cornstarch, and baking powder, and set aside.
3. Beat the egg whites until they start to hold their shape, then beat in half the sugar to form a fairly stiff meringue. In a separate bowl, but using the same beaters (no need to wash them), beat the egg yolks and the remaining sugar until very thick and pale in color, 3 to 4 minutes. Beat in the vanilla. Using a rubber spatula, lightly fold in the meringue and the flour mixture together in alternate batches, deflating the mixture as little as possible. Divide between the pans and smooth the tops. Bake until the cakes are springy to the touch and an inserted toothpick comes out clean, about 25 minutes. Let cool for 5 minutes in the pans, then unmold and gently peel off the parchment. Let cool completely, right side up, on a wire rack.

4. To assemble: Cream the chestnut spread and butter together, and beat in the rum. Place one of the cakes on a cake rack. Spread with the filling, and top with the other cake. Set the filled cake on an upturned 8-inch cake pan and place on a sheet of aluminum foil. Brush the top and sides with the apricot jam, and let set, about 1 hour. Combine the chocolate and oil in a small bowl, and melt over simmering water. Remove from the heat, and stir in the rum. Pour this glaze over the cake, starting at the center, and tilting the pan it's resting on to spread it evenly over the top. Spread the dripped glaze over the sides. (Try not to disturb the top, as this could affect the sheen.) Let set, and transfer the cake to a flat platter. Keep refrigerated until ready to serve.

Cake Rack Basics

Cake racks have feet that raise a cake off the surface for air circulation; otherwise, steam condensing underneath would make it soggy. If you want an extra-smooth surface for decorating, turn the cake upside down. To cool a cake right side up, you need a second round rack, which you lay lightly over the cake. Then quickly reverse both racks, cake and all, and remove the top one. When decorating a cake with a layer of confectioners' sugar, you can use a round rack like a stencil to leave a striped design. Rectangular 18 × 12-inch racks are best for cooling cookies, cupcakes, and breads.

chocolate éclairs

¼ cup brown rice flour

¼ cup tapioca starch

1 teaspoon sugar

3 tablespoons unsalted butter, cut up

Pinch of fine sea salt

2 large eggs

¾ cup heavy cream

½ teaspoon vanilla extract

3 tablespoons confectioners' sugar

2 ounces 60% to 70% dark chocolate, cut up

2 teaspoons canola oil

:: **Makes 12**

A MIXTURE OF BROWN rice flour and tapioca starch makes this pâte à choux—the eggy pastry dough used to make éclairs and cream puffs—particularly light and tender. You'll need a pastry/decorating bag for squeezing out the long, narrow shapes.

1. Preheat the oven to 400°F. Line a large baking sheet with parchment paper.

2. Sift the rice flour, tapioca starch, and sugar together, and set aside. Combine the butter, salt, and ½ cup water in a small saucepan over medium heat. Bring just to a boil, remove from the heat, and add the flour mixture all at once. Place the pan over low heat, and stir hard with a wooden spoon until the mixture dries out a little and forms a ball, about 1 minute. Remove from the heat. Beat in the eggs, one at a time (the mixture will look lumpy at first, but persevere), until the paste is smooth and just holds its shape, about 2 minutes. Transfer to a pastry bag fitted with a 1-inch tip, and pipe out twelve 3½-inch fingers. Bake for 15 minutes, then reduce the heat to 375°F, and bake for a further 15 minutes. Let cool on a wire rack.

3. Beat the cream until it starts to stiffen, then add the vanilla, and sift the confectioners' sugar on top. Continue beating until soft peaks form.

4. Combine the chocolate and canola oil, and melt over hot water. Stir to make a smooth mixture.

5. Slit the éclairs horizontally, and cover the bottom halves with whipped cream. Dip the rounded side of the tops in the chocolate, and place over the cream. Refrigerate until serving time.

almond and lemon cake

2 cups almond meal, or
   1⅓ cups (6½ ounces)
   whole almonds
4 tablespoons
   cornstarch
½ teaspoon baking
   powder
4 large eggs
¾ cup sugar
Grated zest of 1 lemon
1¼ cups confectioners'
   sugar
2 to 3 tablespoons
   lemon juice

:: **Serves 8**

IN THIS EXTRA-LIGHT CAKE, high-protein ground almonds replace the anonymous white fat and white flour found in most bakery items. The simple lemon glaze makes a tangy texture contrast, but if you prefer, you can dust the top with confectioners' sugar.

1. Preheat the oven to 350°F. Butter the sides of a 9-inch round cake pan, and line the base with a circle of parchment paper.

2. Combine the almond meal, cornstarch, and baking powder, and set aside. (If using whole almonds, grind in batches in an electric coffee mill for a floury texture.)

3. Beat the eggs lightly to combine, then beat in the sugar little by little. Beat at medium-high speed until the mixture reaches the ribbon stage, about 7 minutes. Sprinkle the lemon zest on top, and fold in the almond mixture, one-third at a time. Transfer the batter to the pan and smooth the top.

4. Bake until the cake is golden and shrinks away slightly from the sides of the pan, and an inserted toothpick emerges clean, about 30 minutes. Let cool in the pan for 5 minutes. Run a knife blade around the edge of the cake to loosen it, then turn it out onto a wire rack. Peel off the paper, and let cool upside down, smoothest side uppermost.

5. Place the cake on a sheet of aluminum foil. Sift the confectioners' sugar into a bowl. Add the lemon juice, and beat until smooth, 1 minute or less. Pour over the cake, and smooth into a thin layer with a long knife blade, letting the excess drip over the sides. Let the cake stand until the glaze has set, about 1 hour. Transfer to a flat serving plate.

amaretto cake

½ cup (2 ounces)
  almonds
¼ cup brown rice flour
¼ cup cornstarch
1 teaspoon baking
  powder
6 tablespoons unsalted
  butter, softened
¾ cup sugar
3 large eggs
2 tablespoon amaretto
  liqueur
Confectioners' sugar

:: **Serves 8**

THIS LUXURIOUS ALMOND CAKE flavored with almond liqueur will delight marzipan fans. It goes especially well with poached dried apricots.

1. Preheat the oven to 350°F. Butter the sides of an 8-inch round cake pan, and line the base with a circle of parchment paper.

2. Combine the almonds, rice flour, cornstarch, and baking powder in a food processor, and grind to a fine meal.

3. Place the butter and sugar in a large bowl. Using an electric mixer, beat until light and fluffy. Gradually beat in the eggs, and add the amaretto. Fold in the almond-flour mixture in two batches. Transfer the batter to the cake pan.

4. Bake until the cake is golden, shrinks away slightly from the edge of the pan, and feels springy to a light finger touch, 25 to 30 minutes. Let cool in the pan for 2 minutes, then run a knife blade around the edge of the cake to loosen it. Invert onto a wire rack, and peel off the paper. Let cool completely. Lay a second wire rack over the cake. Dust generously with confectioners' sugar, then lift off the rack, leaving a reverse pattern.

walnut-olive oil sponge cake

THIS LIGHT, DELICATE CAKE is manna from heaven for people who have problems with high cholesterol; they can't believe it contains no butter and no egg yolks. And no wheat flour, of course. Be sure to use a very mild-flavored, buttery-tasting, estate-grown olive oil—L'Estornel and Pons from Spain are both excellent, and marry well with the orange zest and sherry flavorings.

½ cup (2 ounces) walnuts
1 cup brown rice flour
½ cup cornstarch
2 teaspoons baking powder
⅛ teaspoon fine sea salt
¾ cup Eggbeaters or other liquid egg substitute
1 cup sugar
⅓ cup mild, extra virgin olive oil
⅓ cup medium dry (Amontillado) Spanish sherry
Zest of 1 orange
Confectioners' sugar

:: **Serves 10**

1. Preheat the oven to 350°F. Grease the sides of a 9-inch round cake pan lightly with olive oil, and line the base with a circle of parchment paper.

2. Roast the walnuts until just starting to smell fragrant, 5 minutes, and chop finely. Combine the rice flour, cornstarch, baking powder, and salt, and reserve.

3. Beat the Eggbeaters and sugar to the ribbon stage, about 3 minutes. Pour the olive oil and sherry around the edge of the bowl, and fold in. Remove the zest from the orange right over the bowl with a zester, so as not to lose any of the aromatic oil. (Save the fruit for another use.)

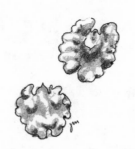

4. Sift the flour mixture over the batter, and fold in. Fold in the walnuts. Spoon the batter into the pan, and bake until an inserted toothpick comes out clean, about 30 minutes. Do not overbake, as this would make the cake dry. Let stand for 10 minutes, then turn out onto a cooling rack. Peel off the paper, turn the cake right side up, and allow to cool completely. Dust with confectioners' sugar before serving.

carrot-ginger cake

A DEPARTURE FROM THE usual carrot cake, this extra-light version lets the natural sweetness of almonds and carrots take center stage, with fresh ginger adding a grace note. A dollop of whipped cream with each slice is optional.

1. Preheat the oven to 350°F. Butter the sides of a 9-inch round cake pan, and line the base with a circle of parchment paper.

2. Combine the carrots, ginger, and lemon zest and juice, and set aside. In a food processor, combine the almonds, rice flour, and baking powder, and process to a fine meal.

3. Using an electric mixer, beat the eggs with the sugar until the mixture reaches the ribbon stage, about 7 minutes. Fluff up the grated carrots with a fork. Spoon around the edges of the bowl, and fold in. Repeat with the almond mixture. Transfer the batter to the pan, and smooth the top. Sprinkle with the pine nuts.

4. Bake until the cake is golden and shrinks away slightly from the sides of the pan, and an inserted toothpick emerges clean, 30 to 35 minutes. Let cool in the pan for 5 minutes. Run a knife blade around the edge of the cake to loosen it, then turn out onto a wire rack. Peel off the parchment paper, reverse onto a second rack, and let cool right side up. Sift a 1-inch wide band of confectioners' sugar around the rim of the cake. Serve with whipped cream, if using.

2 large carrots, finely grated (1½ cups, 6 ounces)

1-inch piece fresh ginger, grated

Juice and minced zest of ½ lemon

1¼ cups (5 ounces) almonds

¼ cup brown rice flour

1 teaspoon baking powder

3 large eggs

⅔ cup sugar

1 tablespoon pine nuts

Confectioners' sugar

Lightly sweetened whipped cream, optional

Serves 10

english fruitcake

12 tablespoons (1½ sticks) unsalted butter, softened

¾ cup packed dark brown sugar

2 large eggs

2 tablespoons Seville orange marmalade

½ cup brown rice flour

½ cup cornstarch

½ teaspoon xanthan gum

1 tablespoon baking powder

½ cup chopped walnuts

¾ cup dried Zante currants

¾ cup dark raisins

½ cup yellow raisins

½ cup dried cherries or chopped prunes, or a mixture of both

½ cup chopped dried figs

3 to 4 tablespoons sliced almonds

:: **Serves 12**

A VERY DIFFERENT KIND of fruitcake, this one resembles a round, low pound cake well studded with walnuts, figs, dried cherries, and what English cooks poetically call "vine fruits." There's no sweet and sticky candied stuff dyed the color of traffic lights, and even the most suspicious find they really like it.

1. Preheat the oven to 325°F. Lightly butter the base and sides of an 8-inch round cake pan, and line with parchment paper, letting the collar extend 1 inch above the rim. (The butter holds the paper in place.)

2. Cream the butter, and beat in the brown sugar, eggs, and marmalade. Beat in the rice flour, cornstarch, xanthan gum, and baking powder to make a smooth mixture. Stir in the walnuts, currants, dark and yellow raisins, cherries, and figs. Transfer to the pan, and smooth the top, mounding it up a little. Sprinkle with the sliced almonds. Bake until firm, about 1 hour, 20 minutes. (If the top starts to brown too quickly, cover lightly with a sheet of aluminum foil.)

A toothpick inserted near the center should emerge clean. Leave in the pan for 10 minutes, then turn out onto a wire rack. Peel off the paper and let cool completely, right side up.

french chocolate mousse

4 ounces 60% to 70%
   dark chocolate, finely
   chopped
1 tablespoon unsalted
   butter, cut up
½ cup Eggbeaters
   or other liquid egg
   substitute
¼ cup sugar
½ teaspoon vanilla
   extract
1 tablespoon brandy
12 Rice Flour Vanilla
   Wafers (page 164)

:: Serves 6

SMOOTH, RICH, AND SILKY, this luscious dessert pairs beautifully with crisp vanilla wafers. As a classic French chocolate mousse is made with raw eggs, I tinkered with tradition because I don't fancy the idea of salmonella poisoning. Happily for us, Eggbeaters (and similar liquid egg substitutes), which are made from 99 percent egg whites, are sterilized and perfectly safe to eat. Serve with the Rice Flour Vanilla Wafers on page 164.

1. Place the chocolate in a small bowl, and melt over hot water. Remove from the heat, add the butter, and stir until smooth. Let cool to lukewarm.
2. Beat the Eggbeaters until slightly thickened, add the sugar, and beat until thick and light, about 2 minutes. Beat in the vanilla and brandy. Pour 1 cup of the mixture over the chocolate, and beat in. Add the chocolate-egg mixture to the remaining Eggbeaters and beat briefly to combine. Spoon into six ½-cup ramekins, cover with plastic wrap, and chill for 2 to 3 hours or overnight. To serve, place each ramekin on a small plate and arrange two vanilla wafers on one side.

quick mango sorbet

FROZEN RIPE MANGO CHUNKS become amazingly rich and creamy when pulverized in a food processor, and turn into a kind of sin-free ice cream. This sorbet is at its best when just made, but can be stored in the freezer. (Cover the surface with plastic wrap to prevent ice crystals from forming.) Frozen mango chunks are available at most natural foods stores, Trader Joe's, and some supermarkets. Serve with the Pine Nut Wafers on page 165.

Drop the frozen mango chunks into a food processor, making sure that all the chunks are separated. Add the sugar and vanilla, and process until very finely ground, scraping the bowl down several times. Add the yogurt, and process briefly until smooth. Spoon into dessert dishes, and angle a pine nut wafer on each side. Serve immediately.

12 ounces frozen mango chunks
2 tablespoons sugar
½ teaspoon vanilla extract
2 tablespoons plain whole milk yogurt

:: **Makes approximately 1 pint; serves 4**

gluten intolerance information/resources ::

NATIONAL SUPPORT GROUPS

American Celiac Society
P.O. Box 23455
New Orleans, LA 70183-0455
e-mail: americanceliacsociety@yahoo.net
www.americanceliacsociety.org

Celiac Disease Foundation
13251 Ventura Boulevard, Suite 1
Studio City, CA 91604
Telephone: 818.990.2354
e-mail: cdf@celiac.org
www.celiac.org

Celiac Sprue Association (CSA/USA)
P.O. Box 31700
Omaha, NE 68131
Telephone: 877.CSA.4CSA
e-mail: celiacs@csaceliacs.org
www.csaceliacs.org

Gluten Intolerance Group of North America (GIG)
15110 10th Avenue SW, Suite A
Seattle, WA 98166-1820
Telephone: 206.246.6652
e-mail: gig@accessone.com
www.gluten.net

R.O.C.K. (Raising Our Celiac Kids)
National support group for parents, families, and friends of kids with celiac disease or gluten intolerance.
www.celiac.com

Canadian Celiac Association
5170 Dixie Road, Suite 204
Mississauga, ON L4W 1E3
Telephone: 800.363.7296
www.celiac.ca

OTHER RESOURCES

Celiac Disease: A Hidden Epidemic, by Peter H. R. Green, M.D., Director of the Celiac Disease Center at Columbia University and Rory Jones (Collins, 2006).
The first authoritative guide on diagnosis, treatment, and management of celiac disease. Essential reading for both patients and the medical community, this is a readable guide to understanding and coping with a serious condition that has been little known until now.

Gluten-Free Living
19A Broadway
Hawthorne, NY 10532
Telephone: 914.741.5420
www.glutenfreeliving.com
A national, full-color magazine with reliable, well-researched information and articles relating to living well with celiac disease.

The Celiac Disease Center at Columbia University, NYC (COCC)
http://www.celiacdiseasecenter.columbia.edu/CF-HOME.htm

The Celiac Sprue Management Clinic at Stanford Hospital
http://stanfordhospital.com/clinicsmedServices/clinics/gastroenterology/celiacSprue.html

mail-order suppliers of gluten-free flours, grains, nuts, and other groceries ::

Bob's Red Mill Natural Foods
5209 SW International Way
Milwaukie, OR 97222
Telephone: 503.654.3215
www.bobsredmill.com

Cream Hill Estates
La Salle, Quebec, Canada
(gluten-free oats)
Telephone: 866.727.3628
www.creamhillestates.com

Empire Chestnut Company
3276 Empire Road SW
Carrollton, OH 44615-9515
www.empirechestnut.com

Ener-G Foods
P.O. Box 84487
Seattle, WA 98124-5787
www.ener-g.com

Gluten-Free Oats Company
578 Lane 9
Powell, WY 82435
Telephone: 307.754.2058
www.glutenfreeoats.com

Gluten-Free Pantry
P.O. Box 840
Glastonbury, CT 06033
Telephone: 800.291.8386
www.glutenfree.com

King Arthur Flour Company
The Baker's Catalogue
P.O. Box 876
Norwich, VT 05055-0876
Telephone: 800.827.6836
e-mail: info@KingArthurFlour.com
www.kingarthurflour.com

The Teff Company
Telephone toll-free: 888-822-2221
e-mail: teffco@earthlink.net
www.teffco.com

acknowledgments

I owe a huge debt of thanks to all those who helped to transform this book from a jumble of recipes into reality. In particular, I'd like to thank Chuck Williams, mentor and friend for over three decades, for wise counsel and encouragement, and my editor at HarperCollins, Harriet Bell, and my literary agent, Carole Bidnick, for having faith in me and for their unfailingly good advice. Last but not least, my thanks go to five tireless recipe testers: Laura Martin Bacon, cookie queen and fellow food-and-cookware writer; Dianne Jacobs, author of the indispensable *Will Write for Food* (Marlowe & Company, 2005); Anna Noelle Rockwell, talented equine artist and fellow dressage rider; Ellen Switkes, indefatigable organizer of the Oakland/San Francisco celiac support group; and Elaine Taylor, cofounder and president of The Taylor Family Foundation, a nonprofit organization that makes an incalculable difference in the lives of sick children.

index